Penguin Masterstudies

Vanity Fair

Graham Handley has taught and lectured for over thirty years. He was Principal
Lecturer in English at the College of All Saints, Tottenham, Research Officer in
English at Birkbeck College, University of London, and is now a part-time
Lecturer with the University of London Department of Extramural Studies. He
has examined at all levels from CSE to Honours Degree, written a number of
literary commentaries and recently edited *Daniel Deronda* for the Clarendon Press,
Oxford.

12420.

Penguin Masterstudies
Advisory Editors: Stephen Coote and Bryan Loug⎵

William Makepeace Thacker⎵

Vanity Fair

Graham Handley, M.A., Ph.D.

Penguin Books

Penguin Books Ltd, Harmondsworth, Middlesex, England
Viking Penguin Inc., 40 West 23rd Street, New York, New York 10010, U.S.A.
Penguin Books Australia Ltd, Ringwood, Victoria, Australia
Penguin Books Canada Ltd, 2801 John Street, Markham, Ontario, Canada L3R 1B4
Penguin Books (N.Z.) Ltd, 182–190 Wairau Road, Auckland 10, New Zealand

First published 1985

Copyright © Graham Handley, 1985
All rights reserved

Made and printed in Great Britain by
Richard Clay (The Chaucer Press) Ltd, Bungay, Suffolk
Filmset in 9/11pt Monophoto Times by
Northumberland Press Ltd, Gateshead, Tyne and Wear

801.953

Contents

Acknowledgements

In addition to the printed sources referred to in the Reading List at the end of this commentary on *Vanity Fair*, I should particularly like to thank Professor Kathleen Tillotson for granting me permission to adapt, as a section heading, the title of her inaugural lecture at Bedford College, London, in 1959, 'The Tale and the Teller'.

Graham Handley

Note: All quotations in this study are taken from the Penguin edition of *Vanity Fair*, edited by J. I. M. Stewart.

. . their way to the City lay through this town of Vanity, they contrived here to set up a fair; a fair wherein should be sold all sorts of vanity, and that it should last all the year long; therefore at this fair are all such merchandise sold, as houses, lands, trades, places, honours, preferments, titles, countries, kingdoms, lusts, pleasures and delights of all sorts, as whores, bawds, wives, husbands, children, masters, servants, lives, blood, bodies, souls, silver, gold, pearls, precious stones, and what not.

And, moreover, at this fair, there is at all times to be seen juggling, cheats, games, plays, fools, apes, knaves, and rogues, and that of every kind.

Here are to be seen too, and that for nothing, thefts, murders, adulteries, false-swearers, and that of a blood-red colour.

John Bunyan, *The Pilgrim's Progress* (1678)

Vanity of vanities, saith the Preacher,
vanity of vanities; all *is* vanity.

Ecclesiastes 1:2

Introduction

Thackeray's Life and Works

William Makepeace Thackeray was born in Calcutta, India, on 18 July 1811. His father, Richmond Thackeray, held a senior position with the East India Company, but he died four years after the birth of the future novelist. His mother decided to stay in India. She subsequently married her first love, now Captain Carmichael-Smyth, and the young Thackeray grew to love his stepfather. He adored his beautiful mother but, following the practice of the time, was sent home to England to be educated. His cousin Richard went with him, and on the way they visited St Helena. It was an experience he was often to recall in later life, for he saw the man who, according to a servant, 'eats three sheep every day, and all the little children he can lay hands on'. The man was Napoleon Bonaparte.

After a short stay at Chiswick Mall, Thackeray was sent with his cousin to a boarding-school in Southampton, where discipline was severe, bullying rampant and the food inadequate. Thackeray was very unhappy there, so much so that he could recall with feeling the anguish he suffered some forty years later. He returned to Chiswick Mall, and already his precocity was evident, manifested in a remarkable talent for drawing and an ability to memorize passages and poems by heart. In 1820 his mother and stepfather returned to England and settled on the Isle of Wight, and in 1822 Thackeray became a boarder at Charterhouse. Like most boys in public schools at this time, Thackeray endured more bullying and had his nose broken. Wounded verbally and physically by the system (he referred to the school as 'Slaughterhouse' in his early writings), he continued to read novels avidly and, despite his short-sightedness and ineptitude at games, he was popular with the other boys. His sense of fun was evident in his comic drawings and satirical verses, his talent for both becoming a lifelong habit.

Before Thackeray went up to Cambridge, he spent nearly a year with his mother and stepfather at Larkbeare in Devon, preparing for his university career by following a somewhat mixed course of reading. He was fond of Scott's Waverley Novels, read the eighteenth-century novelists on whom he was later to lecture, and came to admire the great illustrator George Cruikshank. He had already fallen in love with the theatre and with London life, both passions which were to remain with him throughout his career. In 1829, after his year under parental surveillance, Thackeray entered Trinity College, Cambridge. Soon he was enjoying the literary and social life, and contributed a mock Prize-poem on the subject

11

for that year, 'Timbuctoo' (the prize was won by another undergraduate, Alfred Tennyson). In the vacation he travelled to Paris, nearly got into a scrape with a married woman (he was rescued by his mother), began to gamble, and then returned to a temporarily settled life at Cambridge. There he became friendly with Edward Fitzgerald, the future translator of the *Rubáiyát of Omar Khayyam*, with whom he went to Paris. He soon began to gamble again and succeeded in losing all his money. Thackeray left Cambridge without taking his degree, almost a ruined man.

He persuaded his mother and Major Carmichael-Smyth to let him pursue his studies on the continent. These proved to be of a vague but essentially Bohemian nature, perhaps epitomized by his gaudy appearance at the Grand Ducal Court in Weimar, home of Goethe. Thackeray was later to use many of his experiences there in his Fitz-Boodle writings, as well as in *Vanity Fair.* The stay could not be prolonged and in the summer of 1831 Thackeray was admitted to the Middle Temple to begin his study for the Bar. This part of London was full of literary associations for the impressionable young man: Johnson, Goldsmith and Fielding had all lived and worked in the area. The temptations were many; he was able to indulge his love of the theatre and the roistering company of the taverns, spending and gambling as much as he could, yet constantly the wish to be either journalist, writer or artist – or all three – beset him.

When the Calcutta Bank failed in 1833, what he had left of his fortune was gone and he forsook the law to become a student artist. By the autumn of 1834 Thackeray was in Paris, where his grandmother had decided to settle. He was able to escape from her stern presence to the artists' studios – experiences he was to record in *The Paris Sketch-Book*. He also frequented the literary salons, and it was probably in one of these that he met and fell in love with Isabella Shawe, who had what Ann Monsarrat describes as 'a Gorgon of a mother'. Thackeray now needed to establish himself in order to gain the mother's consent to the marriage. He applied for the position as illustrator for Dickens's *Pickwick Papers* (the original artist, Seymour, had committed suicide), but Dickens did not like his work. Later, as we shall see, there was to be a much more serious conflict between the two men. Meanwhile Thackeray was given the post of Paris correspondent for the magazine the *Constitutional* and, despite the fact that there were already signs of her later mental illness, he married Isabella Shawe in August 1836.

In 1837 the young couple moved to London. On 9 June their first child, Anne Isabella, was born and Thackeray began to earn his living by hectic writing and reviewing. His first story was published in *Bentley's Miscellany* (then edited by Dickens) and he contributed to *The Times* and *Fraser's Magazine.* Thackeray created the character Charles James

Yellowplush, a footman, and wrote a series of his 'reminiscences' with superb comic verve, in eccentric and original language. It gave him a series in *Fraser's* and, despite the demands of the work, reasonable financial security. He was also writing for the *New Monthly Magazine*, inventing a rather different type of hero, Major Gahagan, whose Indian exploits and distorted Irish brogue provided the mainspring of the narratives. Thackeray was also able to present his love of art in a humorous but perceptive fashion, reviewing the art exhibitions in London under the name of Michael Angelo Titmarsh, the pseudonym by which he was most commonly known until his own name supplanted it after the success of *Vanity Fair*.

His first novel, *Catherine*, was serialized in *Fraser's Magazine* in 1839–40. It is a consummate satire of the Newgate school of fiction, exemplified by Bulwer-Lytton's *Paul Clifford*, Harrison Ainsworth's *Rookwood* and Dickens's *Oliver Twist* – in all of which low-life characters play prominent parts. But Thackeray's interest in the eighteenth century and his heroine – a murderess – make *Catherine* an invigorating novel in its own right. Thackeray continued to be a prolific journalist, story-writer and versifier under a number of pseudonyms (*Catherine* was written by 'Ikey Solomons junior'), but private tragedy was close at hand. His second daughter, Jane, died in March 1839 and in 1840 his wife, pregnant again, showed increasing signs of derangement. *The Paris Sketch-Book* was published, and another daughter, Harriet Marian (soon to be known as Minnie), was born in May. A stay at Margate was followed not only by his wife's mental decline, but also by increasing financial difficulties, for both Thackeray and Isabella were poor managers of money. Shortly after he had published *A Shabby Genteel Story*, Isabella tried to commit suicide; by the end of the year (1840) she had been admitted to a nursing home. Various extreme cures were tried, and she had sporadic returns to sanity.

Thackeray continued to work, producing *The Great Hoggarty Diamond* and *The Irish Sketch-Book*, contributing regularly to *Punch* (cartoons, poems, articles) and writing *The Luck of Barry Lyndon*, which was first serialized in *Fraser's*. His was now a bachelor's life, dining out and drinking, both sometimes to excess. He met and fell in love with Jane Brookfield, wife of a minister who had been his contemporary at Cambridge, and visited them frequently, writing her a number of humorous (and poignant) letters. In the summer of 1844 he set out for a tour of the Middle East, resulting in his *Notes of a Journey from Cornhill to Grand Cairo*. *Barry Lyndon* had been a commercial failure, and he began writing 'A Novel without a Hero' in 1845 which, surprisingly, was rejected by some publishers to whom he submitted the early chapters. He continued to supply *Punch* with a variety of articles, among them the brilliant '*Punch*'s Prize Novelists' (later published as *Novels by Eminent Hands*) – parodies in the style of Bulwer-Lytton and Disraeli, as well as of other fashionable novelists of the time.

A short-lived improvement in his wife's health saw her return to England from a sanatorium near Paris later in 1845. He moved to Kensington, mixed in literary circles, and had a succession of nannies-cum-governesses to look after his children. None was completely success-ful, perhaps because Thackeray so loved his daughters – and indeed children generally – that they never met with his approval. Then, at the beginning of 1847 Bradbury and Evans, the proprietors of *Punch* (for whom he continued to work until 1851), began to issue the monthly numbers of *Vanity Fair* which had, as part of its title, *Pen and Pencil Sketches of English Society*. Thackeray's real name appeared on the title page of each number (the novel finished its run in July 1848) and he was contracted to supply the illustrations. As John Sutherland aptly notes, he supplied 'nearly 200 "candles" to his own performance'. Suffice it to say here that *Vanity Fair* made Thackeray's name in his own name, and readers are referred to the section on 'Writing, Publication, Reception'.

The triumph was undermined by living tragedy, for his wife had now become incurably insane. Henceforth he was a public man fêted by the great, giving and returning hospitality, doting on his daughters and, from time to time, brooding on the past and acknowledging the depths of his private grief. His fame brought him more acceptably close to Jane Brookfield. He had thought for some time that his feelings for her were those of a brother, but this convenient self-deception could not be sus-tained indefinitely; he idealized her to the point of telling her that she had at least partly inspired his conception of Amelia in *Vanity Fair*. The Brookfields' marriage had become unhappy, and Jane alternately encouraged, confided in and then repulsed her admirer. When she became pregnant (by her husband), Thackeray was consumed with jealousy; he went to France, where there was a cholera epidemic, only to return to England seriously ill.

By Christmas, however, he was full of the idea of writing a sequel to Sir Walter Scott's *Ivanhoe*, while continuing work on another major novel, *Pendennis*, which had begun to appear in monthly numbers more than a year previously (November 1848). The range of characters, the shifting of scene, the overview of the narrator, the humour as well as a certain inlaid cynicism connect it closely with *Vanity Fair*, but even more closely with its successors in the sequence, *The Newcomes* (1853–5) and *Philip* (1861–2). Shortly after finishing *Pendennis* Thackeray determined that he would lecture on *The English Humorists of the Eighteenth Century*.

After an initial failure through nerves, he attracted large audiences. His writing, too, prospered – *The History of Henry Esmond* was published in 1852. However, in that year he had an unpleasant confrontation with Brookfield and, although they later shook hands, the breach occasioned by Thackeray's love for Jane was never fully healed.

Set in the reign of Queen Anne, *Esmond* is on the one hand a superb historical evocation, bringing to life such figures as Marlborough and Swift, and, on the other, a powerful work of fiction abounding in memorable characters such as Beatrix, Henry and Lady Castlewood. The Brookfields' marriage provided Thackeray with plenty of material for that of the Castlewoods, while Esmond's to the widowed Lady Castlewood, an older woman, caused some disquiet among contemporary reviewers. But *Esmond* was a great success, and increased his claim to stand alongside Dickens as the finest novelist of the age.

Thackeray continued to travel the lecture circuit, and he earned £300 for a performance in Edinburgh. In 1852–3 he delivered his lectures on *The English Humorists of the Eighteenth Century* in America, making about £1,500 in the first few weeks. He fell in love with an attractive young American girl of nineteen called Sally Baxter, but returned to England and proceeded to the continent, staying at Baden Baden, where he began *The Newcomes* – published in twenty-four monthly numbers from October 1853 to August 1855. In *The Newcomes* Thackeray made use of his own Anglo-Indian background, as well as the contemporary ethos of London in its many corrupt and worldly associations; the novel reaches its climax in the pathos of the death of Colonel Newcome, who had lost his fortune and been reduced to extreme poverty. As Ann Monsarrat rightly observes, 'In *Esmond*, he had brought to life a distant age. In *The Newcomes*, he preserved his own for posterity.' He continued travelling widely on the continent with his daughters – Annie, now sixteen, becoming his especial favourite – but he was subject to bouts of ill-health and had to abandon work on *The Newcomes* for some months. He turned aside, however, to write *The Rose and the Ring* – a small masterpiece, nominally for children but enjoyed by generations of adults – which was issued in time for Christmas 1854.

In 1855–6 Thackeray again went to America, this time to lecture on *The Four Georges*, but his health was deteriorating. He suffered from a stricture of the urethra, spasms and attacks of ague, but during 1856–7 he carried on with his lectures in England. Just as Dickens was later to overdo his reading tours, so Thackeray overdid his 'killing and eating the Georges' from Glasgow to Bath. Meanwhile a General Election was approaching, and although he was invited to stand as a candidate for Edinburgh, he declined. Yet in July 1857, after that election, Thackeray stood as an Independent Liberal for Oxford. He was opposed by Edward Cardwell, a future statesman of unquestionable ability, and lost the seat by fifty-five votes. He also lost a great deal of money in electioneering expenses, and realized that he would have to return promptly to writing in order to recoup these losses. The result was *The Virginians*, which was published in twenty-four monthly numbers from November 1857 to October 1859. His suffering became more acute, but he resisted any thought of surgery. Thackeray also suffered from the fear that one or both of his daughters might marry and thus leave him. Annie, the eldest, loved him without question, but Minnie, with something of her father's satirical flair, sometimes criticized the great man who, however, delighted in their company and the fun of their conversation.

The Virginians, an uneven and rambling book, describes the fortunes of the descendants of Colonel Henry Esmond, set both in England and Virginia. Beatrix, now old, has outlived two husbands, and become Baroness Bernstein. The twin brothers, George and Harry, find themselves on opposite sides in the American War of Independence, and historical figures such as General Wolfe and George Washington play some part in the novel. Despite the historical research, it is the entirely fictional Beatrix who dominates the novel.

What became known as the Garrick Club Affair was the next important event in Thackeray's life. It involved Dickens, whose marriage had broken up because of his infatuation with a young actress, Ellen Ternan. Dickens, however, could not bear the gossip this provoked, and issued a statement in his own magazine, *Household Words*, which made no mention of the affair, but stressed the basis of disaffection between himself and Mrs Dickens. Meanwhile Edmund Yates, a friend of Dickens, launched an attack on Thackeray's writings in an insignificant journal called *Town Talk*, accusing him, both as man and writer, of insincerity and hypocrisy. Thackeray replied, taxing Yates with printing his 'private' remarks at the Garrick Club, where they met as gentlemen. Yates took this reply to Dickens who, vulnerable and insecure because of the gossip circulating about himself, dictated a reply which Yates sent to Thackeray. Thackeray sent copies of Yates's article and the correspondence to the Committee of the Garrick Club and from then on the affair escalated. Yates was expelled from the Club and Dickens resigned from its committee in protest. He and Thackeray did not meet until shortly before Thackeray's death in 1863, when Thackeray insisted on shaking hands with him.

Meanwhile the publisher George Smith had conceived the idea of a new monthly magazine, and invited Thackeray to help him plan it. Not only that, he also invited him to become editor of the *Cornhill Magazine*, as it was to be called, on very generous terms. It was launched in January

1860 and among the contributors in the early years, apart from Thackeray, were George Eliot and Anthony Trollope. Tennyson published *Tithonus* in the second number, and Thackeray himself wrote *Philip* as well as *Lovel the Widower*, *The Four Georges* and *Roundabout Papers*.

Thackeray moved to Palace Green, Kensington, where he spent his last years; during that time he was oppressed by the news of the American Civil War, and by the death of Sally Baxter. He began a new story, *Denis Duval*, which was incomplete at his death but which was published posthumously in the *Cornhill*. His daughter Annie (later to become Lady Ritchie) had written *The Story of Elizabeth* before his death, but he was afraid that it would injure him emotionally to read it. In the last few months of 1863 he became increasingly ill and, after several attacks of vomiting and severe pain, he died on 24 December. Annie became a significant minor writer, and Minnie married Leslie Stephen, later editor of *The Dictionary of National Biography*. After her death Stephen married again, one of his daughters being the novelist, Virginia Woolf.

Achievement

In the great age of the English novel, the age of Dickens, George Eliot, the Brontës and, later, the searching and uncompromising Trollope of *The Way We Live Now*, the contribution of Thackeray is individual, various and unique. *Vanity Fair* is one of the greatest novels in our language because of its range, its picture of society, its historical verisimilitude, its compassionate irony, its humour, its pathos and its essential truth to the conditions of life. No other novel that Thackeray wrote reaches the completeness of *Vanity Fair*, but most have their particular enchantments. He could write of history with assurance and power, as in *The History of Henry Esmond* and *The Virginians*, or of his own society with its limitations of evil and perhaps compensatory balances of good in *Pendennis*.

His range in these novels, however, is not as great as that of Dickens. History is more important for Thackeray than the spread of an industrial society around him, while servants, the middle classes and the upper reaches of society – whether commercial or hereditary – are his proper and proven sphere. But if we leave the major novels, though they of course reflect it too, we touch the real quality of the man. While he could dignify the historical novel, he could also parody it, with *Rebecca and Rowena* as the sequel to Scott's *Ivanhoe* perhaps marking the summit of his achievement in this area. Always we are aware of the intense imaginative life of Thackeray, to whom all experience was grist to his literary mill: he saw, he felt, then he wrote or drew it. He was an accomplished versifier, not just in burlesque or parody, though in both these forms he excelled – in verse or prose. *Novels by Eminent Hands*, Thackeray's parodies of some contemporary writers including Disraeli and Bulwer-Lytton, remains not merely readable but funny, and *Catherine* is certainly better in its own right than the 'Newgate' novels which engendered it.

He embraced travel with the zest and anecdotal verve which characterize his work at every turn, and the idea that he was a cynic does not stand the test of familiarity with his writings, both great and small. There is more laughter in Thackeray than there is in Dickens, though it is perhaps present in the minor rather than the major works. Comic journalist extraordinary, his pseudonyms carry the stamp of caricature which he loved to use on footman and earl alike. His satire can be harsh, but there is justice in it. Thackeray is concerned with virtue and vice, but achieves a balance, a perspective, in the presentation of both. When we look at

Becky and Beatrix we look also at what made them, for Thackeray's presentation of character embraces motive and action, sometimes through authorial commentary, sometimes through what the characters say, or what is said about them.

Thackeray's is an upstairs-downstairs world, with the gloss of society and the opportunism of servants exposed to moral scrutiny. Selfishness and worldly advancement are set against virtue and integrity, polar examples being Becky Sharp on the one hand and Colonel Newcome on the other – 'he whose heart was as that of a little child'. But the in-betweens are equally arresting, such as the development of a moral core and some fineness of feeling in Rawdon Crawley, or our gathering recognition that Amelia's ways are more destructive than productive of love. The author is always at our elbow, but the effect is not one of discomfort or intrusion. The distinctive mark of Thackeray's writing is his own presence, whether it be in a light but brilliant piece by Jeames, such as 'SONNICK. Sejested By Prince Halbert Gratiously Killing The Staggs at Sacks-Coburg-Gothy', or by his appraisal of what Jones in his club will think of little Laura Martin's excessive devotion to Amelia when the latter leaves Miss Pinkerton's academy.

When Thackeray digresses, and he does so often, we are aware that it is part of his method to do so, part of his structural control to remind us that we are reading fiction. But these digressions have their counterparts in brief and telling registers of fact, like the closing of Number 9, Chapter 32 of *Vanity Fair*, where the compression raises expectation and points to new directions in the novel:

> Darkness came down on the field and city; and Amelia was praying for George, who was lying on his face, dead, with a bullet through his heart. (p. 386)

Thackeray was a verbal and pictorial artist with pen and pencil – I use the term because it is his own. Sketches, scenes, situations are what he does best, with animation, vivacity, high art, with enough realism to embody truth, enough humour and irony to qualify it and, above all, enough wisdom permanently to enhance the quality of his appraisal.

Literary Influences on Thackeray

There would be little point in trying to summarize the history of English fiction before Thackeray wrote *Vanity Fair*, since dilution is no substitute for reading and experiencing the great novelists in their reality. Thackeray's literary and artistic roots were in the eighteenth century, as his lectures on *The Four Georges* and *The English Humorists of the Eighteenth Century* testify. It is noticeable that both Gay and Hogarth figure prominently in these lectures, taking us beyond fiction and into the areas of theatrical and visual comedy, satire and realism. At one stage, Thackeray even projected writing a history of the reign of Queen Anne, and in his lectures we can see the abiding interest in history which is so apparent in *Vanity Fair*.

The satirical edge of Swift's *Gulliver's Travels*, the humorous whimsicality of Sterne's *Tristram Shandy*, the zest of Fielding's *Tom Jones*, the epistolary modes of Richardson's *Pamela* and perhaps the Waverley Novels of Sir Walter Scott, which Thackeray devoured early on, all seem to have had their influence upon him. Swift, admittedly, he does not appear to be in sympathy with, yet in his lecture on that author he defines what he means by 'humorous' and in doing so possibly defines his own concerns in the writing of fiction:

> The humorous writer professes to awaken and direct your love, your pity, your kindness – your scorn for untruth, pretension, imposture – your tenderness for the weak, the poor, the oppressed, the unhappy. To the best of his means and ability he comments on all the ordinary actions of life almost . . . Accordingly, as he finds, and speaks, and feels the truth best, we regard him, esteem him – sometimes love him.

We like to think that Thackeray is this 'humorous' writer, and perhaps that he liked to think so himself. If we look at the above quotation carefully, we shall see just how it fits Thackeray and his practice in *Vanity Fair*.

The eighteenth century provided Thackeray with the setting for two of his novels – *Henry Esmond* and *The Virginians*. There is little doubt that the essayist of *Spectator* fame, Joseph Addison, was a kind of model for Thackeray – he calls him 'kind, just, serene, impartial . . . admirably wiser, wittier, calmer, and more instructed than almost every man with whom he met'. However, Thackeray's affinity with Addison is social as well as literary: his description of Addison as 'one of the most resolute club-men of his day' reflects Thackeray's own position and status. As Arthur Pollard has observed, *Esmond* is 'a measured imitation' of Addison's style, a tribute to the writer Thackeray most revered. He also loved Fielding – and of Fielding's heroes, Joseph Andrews the best – yet made no attempt to defend Fielding's frailty in his lecture. Again we note the particular emphasis, the moral tone of Thackeray's praise:

> He has an admirable natural love of truth, the keenest instinctive antipathy to hypocrisy, the happiest satirical gift of laughing it to scorn. His wit is wonderfully wise and detective; it flashes upon a rogue and lightens up a rascal like a policeman's lantern.

Thackeray admired Fielding's boisterous freedom in treating matters of sex, a freedom he himself could only indicate obliquely because of the conventions of the time. To Thackeray he was 'manly', and there is little doubt that Fielding's ironical and satirical verve influenced his own conceptions of the novelist's role.

Thackeray accused Sterne of constantly badgering his readers either to laugh or cry, and of a cloying self-consciousness of which he, Thackeray, disapproved. Despite Walter Bagehot's claim that Sterne was an influence on Thackeray, I believe that the main influences were Addison and Fielding; but we should also look at the contemporary writers parodied and pilloried by Thackeray in *Novels by Eminent Hands*, which first came out as '*Punch*'s Prize Novelists' in 1847, while *Vanity Fair* was still in the course of publication.

Vanity Fair evolved as part of a reaction against the 'Newgate' novels of Ainsworth and Bulwer-Lytton, and the novels of fashionable high society which Thackeray also disliked. Similarly, he attacked the stylistic extravagances of Disraeli, the Irish military novelist Charles Lever (Thackeray's parody being 'Phil Fogarty, a Tale of the Fighting Onety-Oneth') and the historical novels of G. P. R. James, the most prolific of the Scott imitators in the mid-nineteenth century. Looking back to Scott and dismissing those of his contemporaries whose work was essentially second-rate, Thackeray restored to the historical novel a dignity comparable to Scott's, but with a much greater degree of realism.

In a sense Thackeray was also motivated by his contemporaries, and perhaps found the example of Dickens a stimulus and challenge in his own writing. After the ironic *Catherine* – in the manner of his master, Fielding, in *Jonathan Wild* – and *Barry Lyndon*, which also derives in part from Fielding, Thackeray's parodies indicate the serious direction in which he was moving. If he could parody his contemporaries, he could also outdo them and demonstrate that he could write the novel which they could not. Interestingly, as we have seen, Thackeray had applied to illustrate

Pickwick Papers, a novel which marks a departure in the publication of English fiction. It was issued in monthly numbers, despite the low valuation set on this mode of publication by Dickens's contemporaries, such as Bulwer-Lytton and Harrison Ainsworth. For many major Victorian writers *Pickwick* became the model for novel publication, and in some instances it tied illustrator to author. This must have been attractive to Thackeray (considering how interested he was in the great eighteenth-century illustrator Hogarth), particularly as the contract for *Vanity Fair* stipulated that he was to supply the illustrations for his text.

Thus the various eighteenth-century writers, and certainly one great illustrator, gave Thackeray the impetus for his own major work. Given his journalistic experience and his unquestionable talent for 'Pen and Pencil Sketches' one can see the attraction of monthly publication for him. His greatest contemporary, Dickens, had made it both popular and respectable. His own illustrations to *Vanity Fair* repay study, for his visual imagination complements his verbal creativity at every turn. The illustrations are an extension of the text, rather like George Eliot's chapter epigraphs in her later novels. But Thackeray is essentially a moral historian, and the eighteenth-century influences cited in this section, plus his own determination to elevate the historical novel with his sense of realism, are the mainsprings of his writing in *Vanity Fair*.

Vanity Fair

Writing, Publication, Reception

The 'Novel without a Hero', as he called it, was long present in Thackeray's mind, and he probably began work on it early in 1845. For the previous ten years he had turned his hand to anything that came his way; from comic journalism, travel, burlesques, to verses, reviews and minor fiction, to name a few. Certainly some chapters of the novel were submitted to an unreliable publisher called Colburn, though whether they were in their final form is not clear. Thackeray asked for them back in May 1845, and is thought to have sent them to other publishers, who rejected them. But he persevered and succeeded with Bradbury and Evans, the proprietors of *Punch* and publishers of Dickens. The latter's novels were published in monthly numbers – amounting to twenty in all – which comprised thirty-two pages each, and this form of serial publication was proposed for Thackeray's novel. The contract with Bradbury and Evans was signed on 25 January 1847, Thackeray agreeing to supply the text and 'at least Two printed Sheets with Two Etchings on Steel, and as many drawings on wood as may be thought necessary'. For each number he was to be paid £60, though the contract did not state how many numbers there were to be. *Vanity Fair*, as it came to be, would also have his own name on the title page. The demands of this kind of serial publication, with its strict page requirement plus the illustrations, imposed upon him a more severe discipline than he had known with the previous magazine issues of *Catherine* and *Barry Lyndon*.

'"The Novel without a hero" begins to come out in May,' he wrote in March 1846; but the publication was delayed until January 1847, possibly because *Dombey and Son* began to appear in monthly numbers in October 1846. By the end of that year he had written three numbers, conceived in great delight the main title *Vanity Fair*, and used his stay in Brighton to further authenticate the atmosphere of the Regency period which characterizes part of the novel. His letters provide evidence of how he used the domestic crises of life in his novel. Writing to Edward Fitzgerald (30 April 1846) he told him, 'One of the bitterest of all the bitter mortifications you have to endure, will be thus leaving the servants & poor tradesmen with their claims unsatisfied', a statement which anticipates Becky's remorseless practice and Rawdon's suffering in *Vanity Fair*.

Before the first number was published Thackeray wrote jauntily to his mother, 'But my prospects are very much improved and Vanity Fair may make me'; while with that first number issued he told Mrs Norton, 'I am no longer a writer in the Chronicle but author on my own account (please order Vanity Fair of all booksellers)'. The early numbers reflect Thackeray's awareness of the craft needed to maintain suspense, the final words of the first being Jos's 'Gad, I'll pop the question at Vauxhall' (p. 76). The afterthought of introducing Dobbin at the beginning of Number 2 has the effect of delaying the Becky–Jos romance, but of raising expectation; while the end of the second number has Becky being set down at Queen's Crawley, the romance failed but the world, so to speak, all before her (p. 109). Number 3 ends with the enigmatic but loaded statement that Becky was 'a match ... in truth, she was – for father and son too' (p. 145), a brilliantly compressed ambiguity for what is to come. As if this were not enough, Number 4 ends with Becky's dramatic and perhaps unsimulated 'O Sir Pitt! ... O, Sir – I – I'm *married already*' (p. 186). Even the most attentive reader would have to wait for Number 5 to discover who is her husband.

I have selected these early numbers to demonstrate how cunningly Thackeray adjusted his art to win his readers. Writing against the clock, something he had always done, had tightened his narrative awareness, and he admitted in a letter to his mother that he was always thinking 'about Vanity Fair'. As the first numbers came out he noted responses to them, saying 'The women like "Vanity Fair"', but adding, with his usual irony, 'the publishers are quite in good spirits about that venture'. The seriousness of his intentions is movingly conveyed in a letter to Mark Lemon (editor of *Punch*) in February 1847, where he says that he has prayed that 'we may never forget truth & Justice and kindness as the great ends of our profession. There's something of the same strain in Vanity Fair.' The spirit of this remark and his intentions in the novel are spelt out for the reader at the end of Chapter 8 (p. 117).

As Thackeray wrote he had to move backwards and forwards in time, documenting, remembering and integrating the narrative strands. John Sutherland observes that these movements 'are found to be both logical and artistically coherent'. Evidence of this care is found in his letters. He wrote to John Murray in June 1847:

> Three of the heroes of a story I am writing are going to be present this very next number at the battle of Waterloo, whereof you announce a new history by Mr Gleig. If the book is ready (and only awaiting the 18th for publication) would you kindly let me have a copy? Titmarsh at Waterloo will be a very remarkable and brilliant performance, doubtless.

Gordon Ray notes that the battle was in fact not presented until the last chapter of Number 9 in September, but Thackeray, who asserted 'We do not claim to rank among the military novelists' (p. 346) was in fact doing his homework as he wrote. Admittedly he does make errors, and suffers from minor aberrations, but these do not affect the main narrative flow. John Sutherland draws attention to the fact that Dobbin met Amelia when she was a child, and that his clumsiness in upsetting a punch-bowl at her party – remembered by George Osborne rather unkindly (pp. 85–6) – is forgotten by Thackeray. In Number 17, Chapter 59, when Dobbin reveals that it was he who bought the piano for Amelia way back in 1815, he says that he first met Amelia when George brought him to her home to meet 'the Amelia whom he was engaged to' (p. 692). But these slips are rare, and we find him writing to Major Compton in December 1847, 'I want awfully to see you – and to-night if poss – I have a chapter about Madras in V F and dont want to make any blunders.'

Thackeray's comments on the novel as it came out are also revealing, and of great importance for modern readers, since his own overview of his 'puppets' is a sure index to the deepening characterization he was achieving. After the appearance of the seventh number, he tells his mother (July 1847):

> Of course you are quite right about Vanity Fair and Amelia being selfish – it is mentioned in this very number. My object is not to make a perfect character or anything like it. Dont you see how odious all the people are in the book (with the exception of Dobbin) – behind whom all there lies a dark moral I hope. What I want is to make a set of people living without God in the world (only that is a cant phrase) greedy pompous mean perfectly self-satisfied for the most part and at ease about their superior virtue. Dobbin and poor Briggs are the only two people with real humility as yet. Amelia's is to come, when her scoundrel of a husband is well dead with a ball in his odious bowels; when she has had sufferings, a child, and a religion – But she has at present a quality above most people whizz: LOVE – by which she shall be saved.

Near the end of the run of *Vanity Fair* he knew just how much he had achieved, telling his mother in jocular (though serious) terms, 'I am become a sort of great man in my way – all but at the top of the tree: indeed there if the truth were known and having a great fight up there with Dickens' (January 1848). Ironically, Thackeray's own personal fight with his rival was yet to come. Still, he was concerned about the fact that 'The book doesn't pay yet with all its unquestionable success', and mentions this fact twice more in March and May 1848. His earlier comments on his characters are reinforced by one made to his mother in May when he observes 'I dislike everybody in the book except Dob: & poor Amelia.' The novel was finished on 29 June 1848 and, conscious of his ambivalent feelings for Jane Brookfield, he wrote to her the next day saying, 'You know you are only a piece of Amelia.'

The first one-volume edition of *Vanity Fair* came out on 18 July 1848 and, as J. I. M. Stewart notes, Thackeray's last corrections were for the cheap edition of 1853. But even after he had completed the work he continued to live the lives of the characters he had created. Ten days after the issue of the novel in volume form he wrote to Jane Brookfield from Brussels:

> I am going today to the Hotel de la Terrasse where Becky used to live, and shall pass by Captain Osborne's lodgings where I recollect meeting him and his little wife who has married again somebody told me: but it is always the way with the grandes passions. Mrs Dobbins or some such name she is now: always an overrated woman I thought – How curious it is! I believe perfectly in all those people & feel quite an interest in the Inn in which they lived.

The mixture of humour and nostalgia with which this is written provides yet another insight into Thackeray; it is as if the flippancy can't disguise the love he feels for what he has created. This love is expressed in another letter, written in May 1848, to the Duke of Devonshire. It exemplifies what most of us feel when we close the final pages of a great novel, particularly those of the nineteenth century: we wish to know, in greater depth, what happened to those fictitious lives we have lived as fully as our own.

In the letter Thackeray tells us that Becky resides in Belgravia, 'conspicuous for her numerous charities, which always get into the newspapers, and her unaffected piety'. Her son, Sir Rawdon Crawley, never sees his mother who is, according to opinion here and at the end of the novel, 'a *most injured woman*'. Becky now wears 'false hair and teeth (the latter give her rather a ghastly look when she smiles)'. Amelia, Dobbin, 'Captain and Lt.-Colonel G. Sedley Osborne', Lady O'Dowd and the indefatigable Glorvina are all touched on, but the second postscript has the final word on Becky:

> The India Mail just arrived announces the utter ruin of the Union Bank of Calcutta, in which all Mrs Crawley's money was. Will Fate never cease to persecute that suffering saint?

This letter was written *before* publication in numbers had come to an end, and the interested reader would do well to look at the last chapter of the novel (and particularly pp. 796–7) for the final version of events. The fun and sweep of the letter are reduced to a singular but ironic reticence; a silent later meeting between Becky, Amelia and Dobbin is followed by Amelia's regretful acknowledgement that Dobbin is fonder of his 'History of the Punjaub' than he is of her. It is the last ironic comment on character and self-recognition in the novel. The vivacity of the letter has been toned down by the artist's conscious responsibility and maturity. He wryly told his mother, when he had finished writing *Vanity Fair*, that it was 'as if the backbone of your stays were out'.

Most reviews of *Vanity Fair* as it appeared were favourable and, as already noted, Thackeray was transformed in the course of a few months from a commercial writer into the major novelist he had so wished to become. One reviewer called him 'the Fielding of the nineteenth century', Charlotte Brontë disagreed with this view and dedicated the second edition of *Jane Eyre* to him because 'I regard him as the first social regenerator of the day'. Mrs Carlyle's famous remark of *Vanity Fair* that it 'beats Dickens out of the world' was not shared by Thackeray. His reaction to the death of Paul Dombey in *Dombey and Son* has passed into literary lore:

There! read that. There is no writing against such power as this – no one has a chance. Read the description of young Paul's death; it is unsurpassed – it is stupendous.

But he was now a great writer, and was treated as such. Although he had deplored the fact that the serialized edition of *Vanity Fair* did not sell well, it was a success in book form, and he eventually made about £2,000 from it. Gordon Ray quotes from another contemporary critic who said, 'He could not have painted Vanity Fair as he has, unless Eden had been shining brightly in his inner eyes.' Ray's own assertion that 'at the lowest estimate *Vanity Fair* is a powerful embodiment of one of the great recurrent responses to life' (perhaps best exemplified in the concluding sentences of the novel, with their stress on happiness, desire and satisfaction – each with a question-mark), is the mark of comprehensive appreciation. At the highest estimate *Vanity Fair* is as rich, as complex, as miscellaneous and frustrating, as life itself. The following pages will seek to demonstrate the many faceted nature of its greatness, both in the particular and the general, and reference will be made in passing to critical appraisals which seem, to this writer, to have brought out the unique qualities present in *Vanity Fair*.

Summary of Plot and Action, with Critical Commentary

As we have seen, *Vanity Fair* was issued in monthly numbers from January 1847 until July 1848 before being published in single volume form. I have chosen to summarize each number briefly in order to put the modern reader in the same position as the first readers of the novel, who had to wait each month to see how the plot would develop, which characters would receive the most space and how the narrative pace of the novel would be sustained by expectation and crisis. Each number had 32 pages, was illustrated (by Thackeray), and cost one shilling, with the last double number occupying 64 pages. This mode of publication put strains upon the writer – who had to keep the tension of expectation high – but also allowed Thackeray to digest comments from friends and critics after each number appeared. Moreover each number, while forming part of the larger whole, had also to be complete in itself in order to hold the reader's interest. I believe that by following the number publication in the succeeding pages we can get a fuller picture of Thackeray's artistic concerns, his narrative directions and the broad historical and moral sweep as it unfolds. The purpose of the accompanying commentary to each number is to indicate these directions, and thence point the reader towards a deeper appreciation of the work's artistic coherence.

1 (Chapters 1–4)

Amelia Sedley, daughter of a City merchant, leaves Miss Pinkerton's academy accompanied by her friend Becky Sharp, an articled pupil who has helped with the teaching. She stays with Amelia at the family home in Russell Square, where she meets Amelia's brother Joseph and immediately sets out to ensnare him. Jos, on leave from India where he is the Collector of Boggley Wollah in the East India Company's Civil Service, is a gourmet, very fat, and excessively shy. Becky flatters and humours him, sings a plaintive song and moves 'the sentimental youth' (p. 75), watched sympathetically by Amelia and critically by her fiancé, George Osborne, a conceited young officer whose father and Amelia's have been business friends for years. Jos determines to propose to Becky.

This opening number is full of typical Thackerayan humour, satire and observation. It also reveals two essentials of Thackeray's style: the creation of an historical milieu through contemporary references and the extensive use of the omniscient narrator. There is the indictment of snobbery in Miss Pinkerton who 'did not understand French; she only directed those who did' (p. 44). Thackeray asserts that Amelia 'is not a heroine' (p. 43), perhaps a subtle preparation for her fuller, yet frailer character later. There are two chapter headings which show his awareness of structure – 'In Which Miss Sharp and Miss Sedley Prepare to Open the Campaign' (p. 46) and 'Rebecca is in Presence of the Enemy' (p. 55). The military tone reflects the excitement of the period (1812–13) in the wake of Napoleon's Russian campaign, and anticipates the wider military emphasis and its repercussions in the Waterloo chapters. Thackeray often employs retrospect, here effectively on Becky, integrating her character from the outset, so that her 'I'm no angel' remark (p. 47) is soon exemplified in her unscrupulous pursuit of Jos. Retrospect is also employed with contrasting effect on Jos himself. Typical Thackerayan asides enhance the humour of the situation – 'If you had told Sycorax that her son Caliban was as handsome as Apollo, she would have been pleased, witch as she was' (p. 60). The sharpness of Mr Sedley contrasts with his later morbidity. The number ends on a note of narrative expectation, the 'make 'em wait' criterion for serial success.

2 (Chapters 5–7)

In the second number the narrative switches to Dobbin's fight with Cuff and his subsequent friendship with George Osborne, then back to Russell Square and the projected visit to Vauxhall. Dobbin accompanies the party on the visit, Jos drinks too much rack punch, fails to propose to Becky and goes to Cheltenham. Becky meets Sir Pitt Crawley, by whom she has been engaged as a governess and leaves with him for Queen's Crawley in Hampshire.

Retrospect is used here to introduce Dobbin into the narrative with some irony, for in a sense the 'Novel without a Hero' has one in this unlikely character. Snobbery is again castigated (the attitude towards buying and selling); Dobbin's virtues as a boy, despite his appearance, anticipate his virtues as a man, while the beginning of his unselfish love for Amelia is portrayed. The Vauxhall visit finds Thackeray in a burlesque mood – 'We might have treated this subject in the genteel, or in the romantic, or in the facetious manner' (p. 88) – though his original parodies here were much longer (see John Sutherland's edition of *Vanity Fair*, World's Classics, pp. 893–6). There is delicious comedy as Jos gets

drunk, which is heightened when he is visited the next morning by
Osborne and Dobbin. Becky acts modestly in adversity, even coyly, but
doesn't fool the servants or George Osborne. One of Thackeray's great
grotesques, Sir Pitt Crawley, is introduced. His eccentricities, particularly
his meanness, are satirized bitingly; he is, after all, an MP. Chapter 7 ends
on a note of nostalgia, the author looking back from his own time (late
1846) to a past era when coaches traversed a beloved route:

> Where is the road now, and its merry incidents of life? Is there no Chelsea or
> Greenwich for the old honest pimple-nosed coachmen? I wonder where they are,
> those good fellows? (p. 108)

He even includes a reference to 'old Weller' (Tony, father of Sam, of
Pickwick Papers fame). The focus of the narrative, however, is still on
Becky. Thackeray is already controlling his readers' responses, aware of
the lure of Becky for them – and for him.

3 (Chapters 8–11)

Becky writes to her 'DEAREST, SWEETEST AMELIA' of her initial experiences at Queen's Crawley, where she meets the second Lady Crawley,
her daughters and Sir Pitt's eldest son who is 'as pompous as an under-
taker' (p. 113). The family portraits embrace those mentioned above, with
some detail on Pitt Crawley, the eldest son, and his devotional practices,
as well as Sir Pitt's unmarried half-sister, Miss Crawley, who has money
and is therefore much fawned upon by the family. Becky ensures that she
herself wins over all the members of the family, and before a year has
passed is 'almost mistress of the house when Mr Crawley was absent' (p.
128). We learn too of Rawdon Crawley, Sir Pitt's second son, who has
already 'fought three bloody duels' (p. 131) and is the wealthy Miss
Crawley's favourite. Bute Crawley, Sir Pitt's brother, is a sporting Rector,
while his wife is 'a smart little body' (p 132), ever-alert for news from the
Hall. She learns of Becky's success there and writes to Miss Pinkerton
about her; Becky gives the news of Miss Crawley's arrival to Amelia and
also describes the family's reactions to it. Rawdon Crawley is also given
some space and, at the end of the number, we find that Becky has
succeeded in fascinating the affectedly Radical Miss Crawley on the one
hand and Rawdon on the other.

This third number indicates Thackeray's range. He moves the action
effortlessly from Russell Square to Queen's Crawley, and in four chapters
the reader is as intimate here as in Russell Square society. There is a

careful noting of the passage of time (Becky has been at Queen's Crawley for a year before the end of the number), and Thackeray cunningly employs the epistolary style common in the eighteenth-century novel to convey the atmosphere, the news and the excitement of events. Becky's letter is racy, witty and graphic, showing how *clever* she is. She brings the strange and unhappy establishment alive through the vivacity of her descriptions. The letter is followed by a warm and intimate aside to the reader:

And, as we bring our characters forward, I will ask leave, as a man and a brother, not only to introduce them, but occasionally to step down from the platform, and talk about them: if they are good and kindly, to love them and shake them by the hand: if they are silly, to laugh at them confidentially in the reader's sleeve: if they are wicked and heartless, to abuse them in the strongest terms which politeness admits of. (p. 117)

This is of course the narrator's voice and we should note that it establishes a moral perspective within which to view the characters and that, by implication, it calls for a like response in each of his readers.

The family portraits are laced with irony – having got his 'pretty Rose' (p. 118), Sir Pitt sometimes beats her; at Eton Mr Crawley was known as 'Miss Crawley'. Sometimes Thackeray's irony is replaced by bluntness, as when he describes Sir Pitt, asserting that 'the whole baronetage, peerage, commonage of England, did not contain a more cunning, mean, selfish, foolish, disreputable old man' (p. 123). Thackeray's irony links the court paid to this 'reeling old Silenus' (p. 117) with that paid to wealth, in the form of Miss Crawley, thus sounding one of the dominant themes of the novel – the base worship of rank and money. Again there is historical placing – Miss Crawley had loved St Just and had 'pictures of Mr Fox in every room' (p. 130). The chapter headed 'Arcadian Simplicity' reveals a highly sophisticated irony, for it embraces the cunning of Mrs Crawley, Becky's second letter to Amelia from 'Humdrum Hall' (which outlines the hypocrisy of the family when Miss Crawley comes to visit – p. 136), and Becky's own ability to ingratiate herself with the old lady and enslave Rawdon. The number ends on a note of expectation: what will Becky achieve? In the first eleven chapters of the novel (with the part-exception of 'Dobbin of Ours') Becky has figured prominently, the centre of interest.

4 (Chapters 12–14)

Amelia is sad because George rarely visits her and she goes to see his sisters, while her father becomes gloomier. In the world outside, Napoleon is defeated; Amelia, much relieved, pours out her heart in her letters to George, who writes 'short and soldierlike' replies (p. 154). George keeps his engagement to Amelia secret, and his irresponsible regimental lifestyle is described. His father tries to persuade George to break his engagement to Amelia, since he doesn't like the look of Mr Sedley's affairs. Miss Crawley arrives in town, ill and nursed by Becky. Rawdon visits them every day, having fallen very much in love with Becky. Miss Crawley's health improves, but she remains dependent on Becky. They meet Amelia and she later visits them in Park Lane, accompanied by George – whom Becky patronizes. Amelia realizes that Rawdon loves Becky. Meanwhile, Lady Crawley dies and Sir Pitt hurriedly summons Becky to Queen's Crawley 'as Lady Crawley, if you like' (p. 185). Becky, greatly moved, reveals that she is already married.

The switch back to London is accomplished with the now-familiar irony, which plays over the Misses Osbornes' condescension to Amelia, the selfish indulgence of George and the importance of the historical events – the battle of Leipsic and the overthrow of Napoleon, 1813–14 (p. 151). The pretensions of society, particularly marriages for money, are satirized in the passing reference to Miss Trotter marrying Lord Methuselah, with the title of the novel well in mind – 'There were half the carriages of Vanity Fair at the wedding' (p. 152). Again Thackeray emphasizes that Amelia 'wasn't a heroine' (p. 154); his characterization of her as sentimental and without a will of her own forms a major contrast with her later actions. Dobbin's devotion to Amelia – selfless devotion at this stage – is shown in his urging George to see her and honour his engagement. Mr Osborne senior is revealed as an irascible and obdurate man, conscious of his rise in Vanity Fair and unscrupulous in his dealings, hence his attempt to get George to break off the match with Amelia.

Becky's return to London and the deposition of Miss Briggs, from Miss Crawley's favour indicates her own steady rise in Vanity Fair. Rawdon's love for Becky is given impetus by Mrs Bute's warning that Becky will be his 'mother-in-law' one day – a masterly narrative stroke which prepares for the climax at the end of the number. The occasional military image – 'Skirmishes of this sort ... the little campaign ... The Crawley heavy cavalry was maddened by defeat, and routed every day' (p. 175) – shows Thackeray linking the personal with the general, namely the battle of Waterloo which is to come. Thackeray's own satirical campaign shows Miss Crawley condescending to Amelia, Becky routing George, and Rawdon mounting his own gambling offensive to fleece the conceited young captain. Meanwhile there is the pathos of Lady Crawley's death, Sir Pitt's insensitive reaction in his immediate proposal to Becky ('the old man fell down on his knees and leered at her like a satyr'(p. 186), and the superb dramatic climax of Becky's revelation.

5 (Chapters 15–18)

Becky rejects Sir Pitt, to the amazement of Miss Crawley, admits to a secret attachment and writes to Rawdon – here called 'Miss Eliza Styles' – who is already her husband. They hire lodgings near Brompton, Becky writes the news of her marriage to Briggs, and Mrs Bute Crawley arrives to visit Miss Crawley. The latter has hysterics when she learns that Rawdon and Becky are man and wife, and old Sir Pitt wrecks Becky's room at Queen's Crawley in his frustration. John Sedley is ruined and sold up; Dobbin buys Amelia's old piano and has it sent to the house in Fulham where the Sedleys now live. At the same auction Becky and Rawdon buy the painting of Jos on an elephant. The last chapter of the number describes the ruin of the Sedleys in terms of its domestic impact, with old Osborne being particularly vindictive and forbidding George to see Amelia. News of Napoleon's escape dominates the wider world; in Amelia's small one, Dobbin again persuades George to do the right thing, and he goes to visit her.

Becky's cunning and resilience, Miss Crawley's snobbery and hypocrisy and Becky's regret that she didn't wait for Lady Crawley to die, are all given a considered stress. The narrative now moves at some pace; Becky's secret is soon revealed in yet another letter – this time to Briggs – and dramatic event follows dramatic event. The sale of the Sedley possessions, Becky's flippancy contrasting with Dobbin's devotion, is followed by a retrospective chapter which describes Sedley's fall. By another stroke of irony, Thackeray has Amelia think that George sent her the piano – another link in the chain of Amelia's illusions, not to be broken until much later.

Apart from the underlying morality – characters portrayed as hypocritical, insensitive, vindictive, irresponsible, flippant, unscrupulous, scheming and false – there is an emphasis on virtue, unselfishness, love, considerateness (largely in Dobbin), pathetic loyalty and love (Amelia), which gives some balance to Vanity Fair, where the author admits to being himself at 'an evening party' and seeing 'Old Miss Toady' flattering 'little Mrs Briefless' (p. 193). But behind the financial crash is the threat of a greater tragedy to come. This is given an impressively documented historical crescendo, perhaps best summed up by Thackeray himself in a sentence which unifies the lives of the small with those of the great:

So imprisoned and tortured was this gentle little heart [Amelia's], when in the month of March, Anno Domini 1815, Napoleon landed at Cannes, and Louis XVIII fled, and all Europe was in alarm, and the funds fell, and old John Sedley was ruined. (p. 216)

The hundred days had begun and, ironically, they are Amelia's hundred days as well.

6 (Chapters 19–22)

Mrs Bute Crawley takes command of Miss Crawley's house, her regime severe and restrictive, and collects details of Rawdon's and Becky's misdemeanours to retail to the sick old woman. The latter, out driving with Mrs Bute, ignores Becky and Rawdon. With George and Amelia reunited, Dobbin, bent on a speedy marriage between the two, visits old Sedley, who is as much against the match as his enemy, old Osborne. Aided by his daughters, Osborne determines that George shall marry the heiress Miss Swartz (Amelia's devoted school-friend), but George, touched by Miss Swartz's generous allusion to Amelia, reveals the strength of his own feelings. The ensuing row with his father only hardens his resolve to marry Amelia 'to-morrow' (p. 256). At the end of April they are married, Amelia being given away by Jos, since her father won't attend the ceremony. They go to Brighton for their honeymoon, where they meet Rawdon and Becky. Dobbin comes down to tell them that the regiment has been ordered to Belgium.

Narrative tension is sustained throughout this number at varying levels. The narrator's voice assumes a lightly ironic tone, insisting that this is 'only a comedy that the reader pays his money to witness' (p. 229) and maintaining that he merely wishes 'to walk with you through the Fair ... that we should all come home after the flare, and the noise, and the gaiety, and be perfectly miserable in private' (p. 229). Mrs Bute's character is exposed to the 'flare'; the medical attendants discuss their patient – and Becky ('Green eyes, fair skin, pretty figure, famous frontal development' (p. 235)) – while Thackeray subtly indicates that Mrs Bute is overdoing it with Miss Crawley. The pathos of old Sedley's position is stressed, and again it is brilliantly aligned with the effects of Napoleon's escape. Old Osborne's ambition for George to marry Miss Swartz underlines his mercenary code (essential to success in Vanity Fair) and George, who has waxed satirical about the 'perfect Belle Sauvage', is seen in his best light yet when he applauds Miss Swartz's love for Amelia. The latter's capacity for self-absorption is shown by her complete neglect of Dobbin when he visits them, while the brutality of old Osborne is displayed in the bitter row he has with George.

The dating of the marriage, at the end of April, places it scarcely seven weeks away from Waterloo, while the contrast of the sparse wedding itself and the snatched honeymoon in Brighton is effectively climaxed by the news of the regiment being ordered to Belgium. Once more the personal and historical, the small events and the great, are linked in time, but the pathos is reserved for Dobbin. His efforts have succeeded; Amelia has married George, but,

Never since he was a boy had he felt so miserable and so lonely. He longed with a heart-sick yearning for the first few days to be over, that he might see her again. (p. 261)

Dobbin's roles of messenger, protector and provider exemplify the selfless antidotes to the bustling self-seekers of Vanity Fair.

7 (Chapters 23–5)

Dobbin tells Miss Osborne of George's intention to honour his engagement to Amelia, then admits that the couple are already married. He goes to the City to inform Mr Osborne, beginning with the news of the regiment's departure. The announcement of the marriage stuns old Osborne. He goes home, locks himself in his study, takes down his great red Bible, erasing George's name from the flyleaf, and next day makes a new will. Meanwhile departure for Belgium is imminent, and Dobbin makes his own goodbyes. Mr Osborne bans him from his house, and Dobbin goes to Brighton (see the previous number). George gets a letter from his father cutting him off with a mere £2,000. He is bitter, blaming Dobbin, neglects Amelia while he consorts with the Crawleys, and is fleeced by Rawdon. Meanwhile Bute Crawley has broken his collarbone, Mrs Bute returns home, Miss Crawley resumes her former habits, Becky meets Briggs and writes Rawdon's farewell letter to his aunt. Miss Crawley sees Rawdon – but not Becky – though he only succeeds in getting twenty pounds out of her.

We note the development in Dobbin's character, apparent in his sounding out of Miss Osborne, with her misreading of his intentions. Dobbin's courage and loyalty are also evinced in his angry exchange with old Osborne. But the finest part of this chapter (24) is found in the detailed examination of old Osborne's character, his dwelling on the past achievements of George (and his pride in them) and the tyrannical obduracy which makes him alter his will. This contrasts poignantly with Dobbin's sympathy for the young Stubble as the soldier writes home to his mother. George's inherent selfishness is stressed in his reactions to his father's letter and his self-indulgence – and blindness – about the Rawdons. Amelia now begins to see through Becky, whose letter in Rawdon's name finds Miss Crawley equal to it. Yet even here the pathos of the situation is sounded, and the narrator's voice prefigures the end of Miss Crawley's role:

> The last scene of her dismal Vanity Fair comedy was fast approaching; the tawdry lamps were going out one by one; and the dark curtain was almost ready to descend. (p. 306)

This grim notation of a useless, lonely life is subtly balanced at the end of the number; for Becky, the little opportunist, enjoys the joke of the twenty pounds, which shows her resilience and self-preserving sense of humour. She has, after all, already ensured that Rawdon will go to Belgium as General Tufto's aide-de-camp, and Thackeray has made sure that the reader knows how quickly time is moving towards the major event of Waterloo: old Osborne's letter to George is dated 7 May.

8 (Chapters 26–9)

George and Amelia go to London and Amelia sees her mother, but also broods on Becky. George draws out the money his father has given him. They go to Chatham, meet the O'Dowds, and Peggy O'Dowd virtually takes over the shy Amelia, who is greatly appreciated by the regiment. Two days after Peggy O'Dowd's party they leave for Ostend, with Jos Sedley accompanying them. Jos is boastful, but George is a little ashamed that his wife has to mix with such low company as the O'Dowds. They arrive at Brussels, and the aristocratic English company there is described, among them General Tufto, accompanied by the Rawdons. Becky soon takes over, the great personages are described and George becomes increasingly attached to Becky, greatly to the discomfort of Amelia. The number ends with the celebrated account of the Duchess of Richmond's ball (15 June 1815) and the part played in it by the main characters of *Vanity Fair*. Finally Dobbin brings news of the French advance and the departure of the regiment 'in three hours' (p. 345); George returns to his room to find a wakeful Amelia waiting for him.

Contrast is of the essence in this fine number, with George's high-life juxtaposed with Amelia's return to the humble simplicity of her home in Fulham. Amelia's character is no longer that of a naïve child-wife; she senses – and this deepens our sympathy for her, yet heightens the drama – that Becky will do her an injury by threatening George's love for her. The whole of this section brings history to life, but more than that, by describing the movement of the fashionable and the aristocratic to Brussels it satirizes the 'Vanity Fair' illusions of war, compared with the terrible reality to come – not least the reality which will affect Amelia. Her simple prayers at home stand out in contrast with George's savage and degrading grasping of his money. Two chapter headings again indicate Thackeray's awareness of structure: Chapter 27, 'In Which Amelia Joins Her Regiment', and Chapter 28, 'In Which Amelia Invades the Low Countries', supply further ironical stress, for Amelia is untypical of those who have invaded.

The historical movement is now emphatic, combining gossip and fact, but including that delightful and experienced campaigner, Peggy O'Dowd, whose kindliness, conversational verve, courage and contempt for what is snobbish and artificial immediately place her as a character who lives outside Vanity Fair. In her Thackeray displays his brilliant gift of mimicry, a wonderful rattling control of an uncontrollable and unforgettable character, and yet another indication of his range. We tend to be swamped by her, and almost overlook Dobbin's continuing protective role as he watches over Amelia (and tries to watch over the feckless George). His reward from the woman he loves so unselfishly is to be smilingly rebuked 'for not having taken any notice of her all night' (p. 322).

The seriousness of the overall situation is briefly relieved through the ridiculing of Jos, but this gives way to a fine piece of scene-setting for Waterloo and the blind confidence everybody shares. Jos, the great coward himself, is articulately patriotic – 'The allies will be in Paris in two months, I tell you' (p. 326). Thackeray provides a fine historical summary (p. 328), but reserves the main barbs of his satire for the way of life in Brussels prior to the battle: 'they found themselves in one of the gayest and most brilliant little capitals in Europe, and where all the Vanity Fair booths were laid out with the most tempting liveliness and splendour' (p. 329). The satire embraces the snobbery of George Osborne, who courts the worthless Bareacres family (note the apt choice of name) and General Tufto – again note the name, though the narrator assures us that 'the General's wig has nothing to do with our story' (p. 331).

Rawdon Crawley is a developing character, and we note that he unaffectedly shakes hands with Amelia. The half-suggested intrigue between Becky and George is now cunningly extended by Thackeray, the irony accentuated as George expresses his relief that 'Rebecca's come: you will have her for a friend, and we may get rid now of this damn'd Irishwoman'

(p. 335). There is no more telling indictment of snobbery and social pretension in the whole of *Vanity Fair* than this simple and hypocritical remark. The night at the Opera – 'It was almost like Old England' (p. 334) – shows Thackeray's satire embracing the public social interplay which covers the private and degrading dealings of individuals, as Rawdon seeks to further entangle George Osborne in debt, and Becky uses the bloodshot General Tufto as cover for her flirtation with George.

Thackeray's own glitter includes an aside at his publishers and an acknowledgement of the reticence he was forced to employ, when he observes of the General's curses 'that I am sure no compositor in Messrs Bradbury and Evans's establishment would venture to print them were they written down' (p. 337). Even Amelia, now caught up in Vanity Fair, assumes a little hypocrisy when she rapturously embraces Becky in public despite her mistrust of the friend who, according to Dobbin, 'writhes and twists about like a snake' (p. 338). But while the moral sin of gambling is castigated between the lines, the sins of display, ostentation and social eminence are treated to a direct authorial definition of what they are in reality:

> There never was, since the days of Darius, such a brilliant train of camp-followers as hung round the Duke of Wellington's army in the Low Countries, in 1815; and led it dancing and feasting, as it were, up to the very brink of battle. (p. 341)

(The ironic reference to Darius is to the great Persian king who also penetrated into Europe before being defeated by the Greeks at Marathon in 490 B.C.)

The scramble for tickets to the Duchess of Richmond's ball has its running ironical accompaniment in Becky's continued condescension to Amelia, the latter's isolation and her knowledge that George is not only flirting with Becky but also gambling. However, it is the flirtation that generates the pathos and the 'note, coiled like a snake among the flowers' (p. 343) which George gives to Becky reminds us of Dobbin's previous snake image. The dramatic news that the troops have only three hours before departure heralds a resurgence of conscience in George; for the first and last time in the novel we respond to him as he repents his treatment of Amelia, writes to his father, and thinks of 'the wife, the child perhaps, from whom unseen he might be about to part' (p. 345). Again it is an unobtrusive touch, but effectively enhances the pathos of the situation. The sweep of history, the convincing linkage of fact with fiction, and the chronicles of the small and the great presented with satirical verve, are the main components of this effectively organized number.

9 (Chapters 30–32)

This section opens with a description of the preparations for the soldiers' departure, concentrating on Peggy O'Dowd, Rawdon and Becky, and then on Dobbin instructing Jos to take care of Amelia when they have gone. Finally George takes leave of Amelia. Jos is left in command of the colony, Becky begins to exert her power over him, and then sees Amelia, who is bitterly resentful of her. Becky asks Peggy O'Dowd to stay with Amelia. Rumours of Napoleon's advance cause Jos to flee, though he has to pay an excessive price for Becky's horses. The wounded begin to come in from the battlefield, and the noise of the Waterloo cannons accelerates Jos's departure. At the end of the number we learn that George Osborne has been killed in action.

The principle of contrast which is inherent in Thackeray's narrative technique is exemplified in Chapter 30 as we note the bravery of Peggy O'Dowd, her genuine love for her husband, the self-interest of Becky (and, in a different way, of Jos), and the anxiety of George to be off to battle, which he regards as another gambling venture. There is an explicit moral focus on those left in Brussels – the determination of Peggy O'Dowd and Amelia to remain, the craven behaviour of Jos, the superb opportunism of Becky and the deliberate promulgation of rumour upon rumour; all this conveys the *atmosphere* of impending battle and the threat of imminent disaster. Selfishness in this Vanity Fair is compared with bravery, with the main emphasis on the contrasting reactions of the women. There is much development of character; for who would have believed that Amelia would have the spirit to confront Becky, or that Becky would have the generosity to appreciate that spirit, although it is directed against her?

There is rich comedy in the rumours which engender panic or resolution, but the business of Vanity Fair continues, with Becky's unscrupulous bargaining over the horses, servants waiting to take advantage of their masters and Jos putting self before family loyalty. The chapter which closes this number is one of the finest in the novel: Becky's brilliant reduction of the Bareacres – we admire her triumph over superannuated aristocratic snobbery – is followed by detailed descriptions of the wounded being brought in, and both incidents reflect reality and cowardice with consummate irony. It is even more ironic that Ensign Stubble brings news that Major O'Dowd *and* George Osborne are safe. Thackeray conveys the frenetic attempts of the Brussels populace to prepare a welcome for the 'victorious' Emperor, in contrast to Becky, who stitches away her valuables about her person, while Peggy O'Dowd observes her usual Sunday prayers.

Although Thackeray claims that he is not among the 'military novelists', the final section of this number summarizes the last phase of Waterloo in prose which reflects, in its movement and rhythm, the rolling forward of the English troops in battle. The closing sentence – recording George's death – is poignant, for this is only one death among many. It brings home, in what is really a brilliant compression, the reality of war. Again we can only admire the structure and control; Thackeray balances individual life against great historical events with wry humour and an unequivocal realism. In the practicalities of serial writing, there is little doubt that this climax meets two of the criteria for success – 'make 'em cry, make 'em wait'. But what we are most aware of is the humanity of the author as he brings history before us and unerringly exposes the movements and motivations of people caught up in its crises.

10 (Chapters 33–5)

The narrative shifts to Miss Crawley, who receives gifts from Rawdon (now Colonel), in reality worthless trophies picked up by Becky, who also wrote letters in her husband's name. Sir Pitt has made Miss Horrocks his mistress and Mrs Bute sends presents to Miss Crawley, while Mr Pitt Crawley courts Lady Jane Sheepshanks – whose mother arranges to call on Miss Crawley. Pitt ingratiates himself with his old aunt, who dotes on Lady Jane. Mrs Bute decides to send her son James to see if he can make any inroads into Miss Crawley's affections. The boy's love of bloodsports and boxing, and his supposed consumption of quarts of gin, as well as his smoking, see him quickly out of favour with Miss Crawley.

Meanwhile Becky has great success in Paris, now of course occupied by the allies, and in the spring of 1816 gives birth to a son. This enrages Miss Crawley, who settles money on Pitt and Lady Jane when they are married. The Gazette is published, and Sir William Dobbin conveys George's last letter to his father. Osborne has a memorial erected for his son and then travels to Belgium, from where he journeys to the battlefields and to George's grave. He passes Amelia, ignores her, and refuses to listen to Dobbin's pleas on her behalf. Dobbin takes her back to England, where she gives birth to a boy who is the image of George. Having seen her comfortable, Dobbin leaves for foreign service again.

In this number satire is cleverly blended with the pathos of Amelia's circumstances, the wilful obstinacy of Osborne and the loyalty, love and devotion – to the point of self-sacrifice – on the part of Dobbin. The satire centres first around the numerous attempts to propitiate Miss Crawley – from Becky's fake relics, Pitt's calculated introduction of Lady Jane and her fearsome mother (with some brilliant, almost Dickensian irony on the over-zealous religiosity of the family), to Mrs Bute's dispatch of the unfortunate Jim. Becky's ingenuity in establishing herself in post-war Parisian society overturns the usual precedence afforded to desiccated aristocracy ('Lady Bareacres and the chiefs of the English society, stupid and irreproachable females, writhed with anguish at the success of the little upstart Becky, whose poisoned jokes quivered and rankled in their chaste breasts' (pp. 413–14)). Pitt, too, subscribes to the codes of Vanity Fair and marries at Miss Crawley's wish, thus ensuring that he and his wife get the money which Rawdon might have inherited. The dating of the birth of Becky's son is exact – 26 March 1816. This concern with creating historical verisimilitude is further emphasized by references to the Gazette and newspapers of the time. The author's tone is at once compassionate and factual, as befits mention of the results of war:

> Anybody who will take the trouble of looking back to a file of the newspapers of the time, must, even now, feel at second-hand this breathless pause of expectation. The lists of casualties are carried on from day to day: you stop in the midst as in a story which is to be continued in our next. (p. 415)

The irony of this is explicit. Thackeray himself is writing a story of what will in future be treated as a part of literary history, and here he is subtly equating reality with fiction; for people read and live for sensation, and death is merely a statistic for all but those who care.

Chronology continues to be recorded precisely, with Sir William Dobbin's visit to old Osborne early in July (1815) – Thackeray is again employing retrospect. About 'two months afterwards' (p. 418) Osborne's daughters see the monument to their brother, and 'towards the end of the autumn' (p. 419) Osborne goes to Belgium. His rejection of Dobbin's plea that he should help Amelia as it was his son's wish is one of the darkest moments in *Vanity Fair*. Though pathos is always attendant upon Amelia, we should note her blindness with regard to Dobbin's worth and the complete devotion she gives to her child. Thackeray's phrase as Dobbin leaves Amelia is a further insight into her selfishness – 'The cruellest looks could not have wounded him more than that glance of hopeless kindness' (p. 426).

11 (Chapters 36–8)

Chapter 36 examines the fortunes of the Rawdon Crawleys from Paris to London, with particular emphasis on the Colonel's skilful gambling – they owe money in both cities. Miss Crawley dies, Becky deals with their creditors and they settle in Mayfair. The continuing account shows them swindling their servants and tradesmen and slighted by London society. Miss Crawley's money – only £5,000 to Bute and £100 to Rawdon – leads, through the cunning of Becky, to a near reconciliation between the brothers. Meanwhile Lord Steyne enters their lives (Rawdon is rapidly becoming known as 'Mrs Crawley's husband') and little Rawdon is neglected, though his father grows to love him. One day Rawdon and his son meet old Sedley with little George Osborne. Jos has returned to India, paying a yearly allowance to his parents, and Mrs Sedley and Amelia are a little jealous of one another over young George, which leads to a bitter quarrel. Amelia's popularity with the opposite sex is described and she receives a proposal from Mr Binny, a local curate, but is too devoted to the memory of George to consider any offers. Dobbin has made some secret provision for Amelia and continues to worship her in India, where he receives occasional letters from her. She is visited by the Major's sisters, who tell her that William will almost certainly marry Glorvina O'Dowd.

The ironical tone of Chapter 36 is implicit in its title – 'How to Live Well on Nothing a Year', Thackeray retrospectively narrates the life of the Rawdon Crawleys in Paris, emphasizing Becky's cunning in urging young officers not to gamble with her husband, which of course only makes them more keen to do so. The decadent Paris society is reflected in the near duel between Colonel O'Dowd and Rawdon, and Becky decides to move the location of her Vanity Fair back to London. The narrative shifts again to chart the growth of little Rawdon, who prefers his nurse to his mother – whom he only sees rarely. This provides another moral comment on Becky and a point of contrast between herself and Amelia. A further moral comment is implicitly made on the swindling of servants and tradesmen, a contrast again with the simple but respectable lives of the Sedleys. A bitter climax is reached in the fate of Raggles, who lets his house to the Rawdon Crawleys and eventually finds himself

driven into the Fleet Prison; yet somebody must pay even for gentlemen who live for nothing a year – and so it was this unlucky Raggles was made the representative of Colonel Crawley's defective capital. (p. 438)

There follows an analysis of the gradations of fashionable society and the snobberies of Vanity Fair, especially among the women, which cause

Becky to be denied access to the great houses. Becky, however, has wit enough to believe that she will be able to use her sister-in-law, Lady Jane, as her sponsor into the best society. The portrait of Lord Steyne is a savage caricature, and that of Becky sexually alluring. The development in Rawdon's character is convincingly achieved. Those elements of fundamental decency which we witnessed earlier are here extended: 'Mrs Crawley's husband' is devoted to his son and frightened of his wife. When Becky comes to see her son she does so with an aura of glamour, but devoid of humanity.

The meeting between little Rawdon and little George reflects the structural coherence within which Thackeray is working. Just as their mothers and fathers have run on parallel – and sometimes opposite – lines, so their movements are mirrored in the innocent coming together of their children. We have seen the upstairs-downstairs interaction in Mayfair, and we now see suburban domesticity in the possessive love of Amelia for little George and the quarrel with her mother. This is an extension of her confrontation with Becky when, we remember, she showed plenty of spirit; but it is also pathetic, since apart from the child she has no other focus of love. Thackeray shows keen insight into the mother–daughter relationship. He also keeps up the running historical documentation of these small lives, with Amelia always observing her wedding anniversary (which we now learn is on 25 April), writing prospectuses for her father and teaching little George.

Mrs Sedley, with more insight than we had hitherto given her credit for, wishes that Amelia would consider Dobbin – though this is largely on the strength of his gift of an expensive shawl. When little George is six years old (i.e. in 1822) Dobbin has him measured for a suit of clothes. Thackeray reveals a touch of irony when he has Amelia kiss little George 'with an extraordinary tenderness' (p. 466) in reaction to hearing the news of Dobbin's supposedly imminent marriage to Glorvina.

Chronological accuracy and character development – plus the narrative interest always felt when Becky is operating – are the main aspects of this number, which serves largely to indicate the passage of time and also to display its effects on the various characters.

12 (Chapters 39–42)

The interaction between Mrs Bute and Sir Pitt at the Hall is described, followed by Sir Pitt's dubious welcome of Lady Jane. In his house Miss Horrocks now rules, but Sir Pitt has a stroke, Mrs Bute enters the house, and the Horrockses are expelled by her energy. The Baronet lingers on for a few months. Lady Southdown, indefatigable zealot, now takes over, Sir Pitt dies and the new Sir Pitt writes informing Rawdon of his father's death. Becky says she will go to the funeral (she has now taken on the late Miss Crawley's old companion, Briggs), where she is affectionately greeted by Lady Jane. Becky affects to dote on Lady Jane's children, ingratiates herself with Lady Southdown at the expense of enduring tracts and sermons, and makes a very favourable impression on the new Sir Pitt. Yet Becky herself feels 'the Vanity of human affairs' (p. 496), sensing that though she is bored at Queen's Crawley there is something pure in its atmosphere.

Next we are brought up to date on the Osborne family, with Frederick Bullock marrying Maria – though he only gets £20,000 with her – and Maria soon learning to patronize her father. There is some detail on the elder sister, Jane, who had once loved a portrait painter, but her father had turned him out of the house. Amelia writes to William to congratulate him on his coming marriage to Glorvina, and Jane Osborne sees little George when he visits the Misses Dobbin and, greatly moved, tells her father.

The irony here plays on the retrenchment of Mrs Bute, Sir Pitt's reception of Lady Jane, and continues an upstairs-downstairs interaction by describing Sir Pitt's degrading behaviour before his stroke, with the elevation of Miss Horrocks to housekeeper. The grim comedy of this is seen in the little servant-girl's praise of Miss Horrocks's singing – ' "Lor, Mum, 'tis bittiful," ' – just like a genteel sycophant in a real drawing-room' (p. 473). There is a noticeable acceleration in the narrative when Mrs Bute takes over, with a convincing control of the dialogue. Pitt's own rise to power adds obduracy to his dullness; he stands up to Lady Southdown, writes his rehearsed letter to Rawdon, and ensures through his family that Becky again moves upwards in Vanity Fair. Becky's reaction to Sir Pitt's death is predictably outrageous – 'I might have been Silenus's widow' (p. 483) – but her manoeuvring on another level brings her success too, and she adopts Briggs as 'house-dog' to guard her own reputation.

Thackeray is thus indicating between the lines the intrigue with Lord Steyne which is later to provide one of the great dramatic climaxes of the novel. The spotlight is very much on Becky as she again ingratiates herself at the Hall (note again the exact historical dating, as Miss Rosalind says 'She's hardly changed since eight years' (p. 488), while Pitt's letter to his brother was written on 14 September 1822 (p. 480)). The running humour covers Becky's hypocritical attention to Lady Southdown's tracts, and her own suffering on 'Lady Macbeth's' account from the latter's medication. Becky's later recital of 'Lady Southdown and the black dose' (p.

491) shows just what an accomplished little actress she is. The author's description of Sir Pitt's funeral ends with the biting comment that

As long as we have a man's body, we play our Vanities upon it, surrounding it with humbug and ceremonies, laying it in state, and packing it up in gilt nails and velvet: and we finish our duty by placing over it a stone, written all over with lies. (p. 493)

Truly we are in Vanity Fair, and Becky's imagination is seen working on the possibilities of a country life, but 'she was committed to the other path, from which retreat was now impossible' (p. 497).

The return to London is marked by a satirical account of the Bullock–Maria Osborne wedding, the snobbery of the married sister, and then turns to the pathos of Jane Osborne's lot – her unhappy love affair and the tyranny of old Osborne in insisting that she shall not marry. Her own deprivation accounts for her breakdown in front of her father after she has seen little George – even Thackeray's minor characters are given a degree of psychological consistency – while Amelia's letter to Dobbin contains the unvoiced irony that now she thinks Dobbin is about to be married, she begins to value him.

13 (Chapters 43–6)

The opening chapter transports us to Bundlegunge in Madras, with Glorvina intent on Dobbin. Dobbin receives Amelia's letter, then one from his sister which suggests that Amelia may marry Mr Binny, and decides to get leave and go to England. Meanwhile Becky supervises the renovation of the Crawleys' old house in Gaunt Street, completely wins over the new Sir Pitt but gets no money out of him, and begins to hate little Rawdon – as does Lord Steyne. The Rawdon Crawleys spend Christmas in Hampshire where Lady Jane is kind to the little boy and Becky makes further attempts to ingratiate herself with Sir Pitt. The latter gives Rawdon £100. Becky despises Lady Jane for her naïve goodness, and later caricatures her pompous brother-in-law for Lord Steyne.

Old Osborne formally offers to take little Georgy and to maintain Amelia's allowance should she decide to marry again. Amelia is deeply angry, but soon finds her family in serious financial difficulties. She sells the shawl Dobbin gave her, buys books for Georgy and then, reprimanded by her mother since they have no food, gives her the rest of the money and breaks down, feeling that she is sacrificing her son to her own selfish interests.

The comedy of Glorvina's attempts on Dobbin is complemented by his clear insight into her nature – 'she is only keeping her hand in' (p. 509), he believes, by practising on him. Major O'Dowd shows his own integrity by refusing to take part in his wife's conspiracy to get Dobbin married. Dobbin's own suffering after he gets Amelia's letter, and even more after he gets his sister's, shows the obstinate loyalty of his devotion to Amelia.

The narrative switch to Curzon Street marks a deepening revelation of Becky's character and, as throughout the novel, its contrast with Amelia's. The latter is a good mother; Becky is a bad one, and her striking of little Rawdon who wants to hear her sing shows her in the worst light. Amelia clings to motherhood, while Becky attempts to free herself from it. The upstairs-downstairs interaction continues with Briggs buying the little boy a coat and the servants talking of Becky's affair with Lord Steyne. There is further contrast at Queen's Crawley; Lady Jane behaves like a mother to little Rawdon and Becky steals the new Sir Pitt, just as she stole George Osborne in the past, but here with mercenary rather than sexual motivation. Sir Pitt is easily duped, and this occasions a running satirical commentary from the narrator. A foxhunt is graphically described – or at least the preparations for it – cunningly seen as if through the eyes of little Rawdon.

There is some pathos in the increasing isolation of Rawdon himself, and Lord Steyne assumes more and more detestable proportions. Thackeray uses Rawdon for another chronological indication – 'The bold and reckless young blood of tên years back was subjugated, and was turned into a torpid, submissive, middle-aged, stout gentleman' (p. 536). The number ends with one more telling contrast – the needs of Amelia and her family. Amelia misguidedly sacrifices herself for her child at the expense of her mother and father, sorely distressed at the thought that little George could have a better life with old Osborne. Thackeray finishes this number on a note of narrative pathos *and* tension – will Amelia give in to Mr Osborne's demands? When will Dobbin arrive? And, more subtly, when will Becky's affair with Lord Steyne be revealed?

14 (Chapters 47–50)

Chapter 47 is devoted to the history of Lord Steyne's family, with an account of the 'taint of the blood' present in Steyne's son and which he fears in himself – insanity. Becky is presented at Court by Sir Pitt, who has, without telling his wife, given her some diamonds for the occasion – Lord Steyne having supplied some of her other jewels. Steyne gives money to Becky, who says that she has ruined Briggs, but Becky merely buys 'the simple old spinster' (p. 565) a dress and gives some of her other creditors money on account. Becky is invited to a dinner at Gaunt House where, although snubbed by most of the ladies, she has 'a great triumph' (p. 573).

Meanwhile Amelia tries to get some teaching work in order to keep little George with her. She learns that her father has imprudently wasted Jos's annuity and makes the decision to part with her son. Driven by their poverty, she writes to Jane Osborne, who shows the letter to her father. George's old room is got ready, Jane Osborne takes Amelia £100, and Amelia tells little George that he is to live with his grandfather. The child is delighted and visits his mother occasionally, while Amelia often walks to Russell Square and silently watches for the sight of him.

The account of Gaunt House and the history of Lord Steyne's family is written in Thackeray's best mock-heroic style, and is underpinned by the author's supposed informant, Tom Eaves, with the choicer pieces of gossip. The satirical approach stresses the title of the novel, for all in Vanity Fair, including Sir Pitt Crawley, pay court to this corrupt, degraded, loathsome man whose only possession is rank and whose moral obloquy is such that he terrorizes his womenfolk. Becky's presentation at Court is also given the full satirical treatment:

What were the circumstances of the interview between Rebecca Crawley *née* Sharp, and her Imperial Master, it does not become such a feeble and inexperienced pen as mine to attempt to relate. The dazzled eyes close before that Magnificent Idea. Loyal respect and decency tell even the imagination not to look too keenly and audaciously about the sacred audience chamber, but to back away rapidly, silently, and respectfully, making profound bows out of the August Presence. (pp. 559–60)

Newspaper comment is balanced by the vituperative irony of Mrs Bute, and Becky's power over Lord Steyne is shown in the matter of the cheque.

All this while – and it is a considered omission from the text – we are aware of Rawdon's ignorance of what is going on, and his isolation from Becky's rise in Vanity Fair. The picture of Lord Steyne at home shows the real nature of the man, though outwardly he treats his wife with 'distinguished courtesy' so that the outside world is forced 'to own that his Lordship's heart at least was in the right place' (p. 568). But even in this telling exposure of the mores of high society Thackeray introduces moments of humanity, as when Lord Steyne calls his wife by her Christian name in token of her response to Becky at their Friday dinner.

Again Thackeray employs contrast in Chapter 50, as we move down the social scale, with Amelia's poignant preparations for her son's departure and Georgy's eagerness to leave. As the author laconically observes, 'The boy was the image of his father, as his fond mother thought' (p. 580). The sentimental tone in this final chapter of the number is put into perspective by an admirably realistic comment on the rapid changes wrought by the passage of time:

A few days are past: and the great event of Amelia's life is consummated. No angel has intervened. The child is sacrificed and offered up to fate; and the widow is quite alone. (p. 582)

The finality this embraces is as succinct as the description of the death of George Osborne.

15 (Chapters 51–3)

Becky's rising society career after the dinner at Lord Steyne's, 'when she moved among the very greatest circles of the London fashion' (p. 587), is described. She survives attacks from the ladies, attends the charades at Gaunt House, and acts in them to acclamation. After he has put his wife into her carriage, Rawdon is arrested by the bailiffs for debt. Chapter 52 opens with an account of young Rawdon going to school, much missed by his father but ignored by his mother. Steyne, relieved to get rid of the boy, now makes provision for Briggs also. Becky nearly falls out with Sir Pitt, who warns her about her behaviour. Prior to his arrest, Rawdon has been paying more attention to Becky and taking her for drives; imprisoned at Mr Moss's, he writes to his wife, who replies with emotionally simulated concern but does nothing. Meanwhile the tremulous but good-hearted Lady Jane settles Rawdon's debts. Rawdon walks home, finds Steyne with Becky, calls the peer a coward and a villain, knocks him bleeding to the ground, and takes Becky's keys, asserting that he will pay all their debts and return anything of Lord Steyne's to him. Becky is left alone and, temporarily, desolate.

This number shows Thackeray at his best. The ironic tone is used as commentary on Becky's 'aristocratic pleasures ... for these too, like all other mortal delights, were but transitory' (p. 584). The society she moves in is subjected to numerous satiric shafts, though to be fair to Becky, we are told that 'Her success excited, elated, and then bored her' (p. 587). There is a wonderful paragraph, allegedly from the *Morning Post*, listing the select guests at one of Becky's parties. The description of the charades, and Becky's part in them, reflects the nature of Vanity Fair and symbolizes Becky's worldly role.

To emphasize his theme that all is vanity, Thackeray balances the moment of Becky's greatest triumph with Rawdon's arrest, follows it with the duplicity of Lord Steyne and, in effective retrospect, has Rawdon temporarily ruling his wife as well as wishing that she were a good mother to her boy. The final chapter of the number is one of the highlights of *Vanity Fair*. It moves with speed to a dramatic climax, with Rawdon's developed character as a moral index to the action. There is a fine contrast between Rawdon's misspelt, sincere letter of concern for Becky and her affected (note the French phrases) expression of concern, but no action, in reply. This contrast is further developed in the prompt and unselfish action of Lady Jane.

The climax is superbly constructed; Rawdon's actions upon discovering Becky and Lord Steyne together, are as natural and passionate as blind instinct. Becky's reactions of admiration and fear of her husband are conveyed in the passion of the moment as she continues to assert her innocence. The series of rhetorical questions with which Thackeray closes the scene is accompanied by a definitive statement of moral death:

All her lies and her schemes, all her selfishness and her wiles, all her wit and genius, had come to this bankruptcy. (p. 622)

Around Becky lies the 'heap of tumbled vanities' (p. 622), yet so studied is the writing, so perfect the control, that we feel some compassion for her.

16 (Chapters 54–6)

Rawdon goes to see his brother (he has obviously left Becky for good) and asks him to care for little Rawdon, since he intends to fight a duel with Lord Steyne. He visits Captain Macmurdo, who will be his second, and they write the challenge to Steyne, while the servants take possession of the house in Curzon Street. Becky descends in the afternoon to find them in control, says that Rawdon has made off with £1,500, and promises to pay them all the next day. She goes to see Sir Pitt, throws herself at his feet, is interrupted and berated by a spirited Lady Jane, but persuades Pitt to try and seek a reconciliation for her.

Meanwhile Rawdon learns that he has been appointed to the Governorship of Coventry Island, and Steyne's friend Wenham comes to talk him out of the duel, Steyne having secured the Coventry Island appointment for Rawdon. Macmurdo supports Steyne's emissary, and the affair is hushed up. Raggles is bankrupted, Rawdon goes to Coventry Island and little Rawdon goes to stay with Lady Jane in his holidays. Meanwhile young Georgy is spoiled by Jane Osborne and soon begins to lord it over his ignorant grandfather; he shows all the snobbery and conceit of his father, and his education is described. Mrs Sedley dies, and Dobbin and Jos come to visit little George.

The narrative tension of the previous number is maintained through an affecting interview between Rawdon and Sir Pitt, with the former's concern for his son our main concern too. We are moved by Rawdon's now broken love for Becky, and by Macmurdo's sympathy for him. The upstairs-downstairs interaction is here reduced to grim comedy with the servants' takeover in Curzon Street; Becky, never at a loss, unashamedly goes to Sir Pitt. While Rawdon suffers, Becky improvises. Lady Jane's spirited rejection of Becky (comparable to Amelia's attack on her 'friend' on the eve of Waterloo) underlines one of the main themes of the novel – the confrontation of virtue and vice.

Rawdon's appointment to Coventry Island shows Thackeray's capacity to use the unexpected dramatically; it is also a comment on those who rule in Vanity Fair, where corruption and preferment, the immoral sinecures of the great, are used for their own ends. The introduction of Mr Wenham into the narrative again shows Thackeray's ability to bring to life a minor functional character. Mr Wenham, master of the hypocritical innuendo, claims that he and Mrs Wenham were due to dine with Steyne and Becky on the fated night – which lines his pockets and ensures Steyne's safety. The bankruptcy of Raggles is given a brief mention – an ironic comment on the fact that the world ignores *his* plight as of little importance beside the affairs of aristocrats and commercial tycoons.

There is a certain narrative cunning in the way Becky fades at this time from the story, for the question-mark hanging over her exact whereabouts raises expectation. The contrast between little George and little Rawdon is given a considered stress which is interesting and effective; both are given a family likeness, and perhaps we should note too that each lives in a man's world where the women are completely subordinate. Amelia now receives only the occasional visit from her son, while young Rawdy lives for the hunting in Hampshire. Again the number ends on a note of climax with the arrival of Dobbin. Before that, we have been treated to Thackeray's satirical observations on the nature of Georgy's education.

17 (Chapters 57–60)

Georgy carries money to his mother from old Osborne and Amelia devotes herself to her father. Meanwhile Dobbin, after some delay because of a high fever in which he deliriously raves about Amelia, comes home to England with Jos. He still loves Amelia, and goes straight to Brompton when he arrives. He finds her sitting on a bench with old Sedley, and Amelia is soon boasting to him about the remarkable achievements of her son. Dobbin tells them that Jos will soon be arriving. Jos arrives, ignorant of his mother's death, and is greatly moved. He takes a new house, and Amelia and her father move there from Brompton – Amelia taking with her the old piano which George, as she thinks, bought for her all those years ago. She realizes that Dobbin had in fact made the purchase, and he now confesses his love for her. She regards herself as still married to George, and Dobbin says that he only asks to 'let me stay near you, and see you often' (p. 693). Amelia now starts to move in society again; she is visited by Miss Osborne, the Misses Dobbin, and begins to drive out in her carriage. Jos is thought to have plenty of money, though his nephew, young George, is given to mocking his pomposity.

Mrs Sedley's funeral occupies the first part of this number; but since the focus of the previous one was on Dobbin's arrival, Thackeray employs retrospect to bring us up to date, giving some space to the splendid Jos. The latter is influenced by Dobbin, always concerned for Amelia, to think of setting up an establishment for her and his father when he gets home. The central role of Dobbin in the narrative is maintained, Thackeray conveying Dobbin's mood of joyous anticipation at the thought of seeing Amelia – perhaps best indicated in his reaction as he hurries towards Kensington and passes the married Mr Binny. Both his and Amelia's delusion – that the other has probably married – make for a delightful irony; but whereas Dobbin's leads to his spontaneous confession of love, Amelia's merely leads to her misguidedly calculating a suitable match for him among her friends. When Amelia shows Dobbin Georgy's composition (a remarkable stroke of irony this, since the subject is 'Selfishness', and that young man symbolizes it) it provides us with a precise historical date – 24 April 1827.

Amelia's idolatry with regard to her dead husband diminishes some of our sympathy for her, but it returns when she breaks down and Dobbin 'folded his arms round her, holding her to him as if she was a child' (p. 693). Young George Osborne grows in stature as a character because of his unequivocal liking for Dobbin, and the satirical tone now embraces Amelia's return to 'genteel society'. With Becky absent from the narrative we note that the two heroines' respective fates have come full circle: she is, perhaps temporarily, eclipsed, and Amelia's star has risen – part of the insistent contrast which runs throughout the novel.

18 (Chapters 61–3)

The principle of contrast is carried further in the opening of the next number, which contains the deaths of those early friends and old enemies, Mr Sedley and Mr Osborne. The latter experiences some change of heart before he dies, and leaves Amelia an annuity of £500. More importantly, Amelia is to 'resume the guardianship of the boy' (p. 709). Amelia also learns that it is Dobbin who has supported her and her family hitherto. Maria Bullock, née Osborne, is now reconciled to Amelia (they haven't met for fifteen years), and Amelia finds that she is fully welcomed again in Vanity Fair.

Amelia, Jos, Dobbin and Georgy embark on a continental tour, eventually staying at the little town of Pumpernickel. Gradually Amelia's feelings change towards the faithful Dobbin. They attend the Court and musical entertainments, mix in the highest English society to the delight of the sycophantic Jos, and the setting and pleasures of Pumpernickel are described in some detail. Amelia entertains, and Dobbin tutors Georgy; the latter goes gambling, and a masked woman asks him to put down a coin for her. Later she makes herself known to Jos – 'Madame de Raudon' – reduced to the expedient of gambling. She asks Jos to come away with her, for 'we are old friends, are we not, dear Mr Sedley?' (p. 737).

Old Sedley's death is reticently but movingly depicted. Amelia's nursing of him and his complete dependence on her provide a humanizing quality: when he dies it is 'in that humble frame of mind, and holding by the hand of his daughter, life and disappointment and vanity sank away from under him' (p. 704). The extent of Dobbin's financial support of Amelia and George is ironically discovered by old Osborne, whose softening before death again illustrates the character development typical of Thackeray's technique. In fact Chapter 61 is full of ironies, with some of old Sedley's wine being drunk when Jos and Dobbin are asked to dine with old Osborne. The final touch of generosity in a man who has lived a life of selfishness of spirit is shown in his leaving Dobbin, in gratitude for his kindness to Amelia and little George, enough money to purchase a commission as Lieutenant-Colonel. Too much indulgence of vanity in this case has carried with it a degree of conscience.

Amelia – or Emmy as Thackeray increasingly calls her – rises, but the narrator's comment on the renewal of friendships with her now that she has money, reminds us of the past when she was neglected, for 'Who is ever missed in Vanity Fair?' (p. 712). But Thackeray reserves his finest satire for the trip to Pumpernickel, beginning with a brilliant catalogue of those travellers of importance (in Vanity Fair) on the steamboat and Jos's shameless worshipping of the dyed Bareacres. Arrived 'Am Rhein', the narrator affects to be with the travellers, for 'It was at the little comfortable Ducal town of Pumpernickel ... that I first saw Colonel Dobbin and his party' (p. 721). The effect is one of intimacy with the reader (we know that Thackeray is drawing on his own experiences) and there are some fine touches, particularly those which record Amelia's response to this new life – of music and entertainment – which is opening up before her. Her weeping at *Fidelio* calls forth this aside: 'Every woman in the house was snivelling at the time: but I suppose it was because it was predestined that I was to write this particular lady's memoirs that I remarked her' (p. 722). It is a sly but endearing reminder of the teller in his tale. The not so endearingly named Tapeworm comes in for satirical scrutiny, the authorial 'we' in Chapter 62 being employed as a parody of a casual newspaper report from abroad, and ending with a brief remark about Amelia: 'We rather hoped that nice-looking woman would be induced to stay some time in the town' (p. 725).

Comic names – such as Gräfinn Fanny de Butterbrod – are employed throughout Chapter 63. Thackeray draws on the memories of his stay in Weimar, creates its atmosphere, delights in its snobberies and, intent on getting Becky back into the narrative, its gambling – the vice which was Thackeray's own undoing in his youth. We note that Dobbin's morality allows of no gambling (he makes this clear to Georgy) and as the moral pivot of the novel, he tries to draw Jos away from temptation. But Jos succumbs, Becky is back, and the number ends on the high expectation we have come to expect. Coincidence has been stretched far – nearly all our leading characters are together again by the chance of being in Pumpernickel at the same time – but our interest has been quickened by this cunning sleight of hand on Thackeray's part.

19–20 (Chapters 64–7)

The final number of *Vanity Fair* was a double one, published in July 1848. Chapter 64 comprises a summary of Becky's life prior to her appearance in Pumpernickel. She writes to young Rawdon when he becomes the heir to Queen's Crawley (Lady Jane's son having died), and stays at Boulogne, enduring the snubs of those who once courted her (for such is Vanity Fair). Then she moves on from place to place, from Paris to Brussels, always 'a boarding-house queen' (p. 747). She meets Steyne in Rome by chance, but he ignores her, staring 'aghast at her for a minute, as Macbeth might on beholding Banquo's sudden appearance at his ball-supper'

(p. 751). She is warned to leave Rome, and there follows a notice of the death of Steyne in 1830.

We return to Becky, who is entertaining a student when Jos arrives to see her. He is soon convinced that she has always loved him, tells Dobbin of her presence, and finds Amelia touched by the recital of her troubles. She immediately visits Becky, 'and forgave her at that moment' (p. 762). Becky tells Amelia that little Rawdon has been taken away from her, while Dobbin overhears students talking of Becky. He realizes that she is still 'going on with her intrigues' (p. 767) and is dismayed to learn that Amelia intends to take her into the house. He indignantly leaves the house, walks about the town, goes back the next day and, in front of Becky, tells Amelia that he considers Becky unfit company for her. Amelia replies with spirit and Dobbin speaks to her alone, telling her, 'You are not worthy of the love which I have devoted to you' (p. 776). He leaves, supposedly for good, and young Georgy is very upset.

Becky establishes herself in the house and cunningly gets the portrait of Jos which she and Rawdon had bought at the sale all those years ago. Dobbin becomes a Lieutenant-Colonel, Amelia broods, then Jos, Becky and Amelia move to Ostend, where Amelia is pestered by two of Becky's unscrupulous male friends who know of her designs on Jos. Becky, to do her credit, becomes anxious on Amelia's account, and reveals the truth about the past – her own affair with George Osborne – in order to persuade Amelia to see Dobbin's true worth. She proves George's infidelity by producing the note he had written to her on the night of the Duchess of Richmond's ball.

Amelia has already written to Dobbin; he comes to her, and promises never to leave again. Becky modestly disappears from the scene, and a brief summary covers the O'Dowds, Dobbin leaving the service, Amelia's friendship with Lady Jane, as well as that between George and Rawdon. Jos travels, with Becky always in attendance upon him. He has heavily insured his life and is too frightened of Becky to come home. Jos dies, leaving his money divided between Becky and Amelia. Rawdon Senior and Sir Pitt die within weeks of each other, and Becky 'chiefly hangs about Bath and Cheltenham' (p. 796), where 'She busies herself in works of piety' (p. 796). Meanwhile Dobbin continues to write his 'History of the Punjaub', his wife feeling that kind though he is to her, he perhaps thinks more of his daughter Janey.

The omniscient opening to this double number has a defensive tone, almost as if the writer has overstepped the moral mark in his presentation of Becky. His justification shows how he had to subscribe to the convention of the time:

Those who like may peep down under the waves that are pretty transparent, and see it writhing and twirling, diabolically hideous and slimy, flapping amongst bones, or curling round corpses; but above the water-line, I ask, has not everything been proper, agreeable, and decorous, and has any the most squeamish immoralist in Vanity Fair the right to cry fie? (p. 738)

The retrospective view of Becky, even while it describes her descent in society, always conveys her survival at whatever level of the murky depths.

The meeting with Lord Steyne, and the description of his death in 1830 – where all his titles are brilliantly and satirically listed – once more stresses the interaction of the individual with history by mentioning the French Revolution of that year. Becky's Bohemian existence is depicted with verve, her acting as good as it has ever been, despite the rouge pot and the brandy bottle. We can't help but feel that Jos gets what he deserves, since Becky's return to the plot is essential anyway: she has to be instrumental in bringing Amelia and Dobbin together. Like Rosamond Vincy in *Middlemarch*, who tells Dorothea that Will Ladislaw loves her and not herself (Rosamond), Becky undertakes the one generous action of her life, hard though it is to shatter Amelia's illusions about George.

Before this incident we have the contrast between Dobbin's clear-sightedness and forthrightness and Amelia's foolish sentimentality and misguided pride. The truth is, as Thackeray makes clear, Amelia cannot bear that Dobbin should shatter the illusions that Becky later brings into the open. When he does, by reminding her that Becky was not always her friend, she fiercely rebuffs him, prompting Dobbin to sadly tell her that she has not been worth the devoted love he has given her. Truth comes to Amelia, accompanied by the authorial voice:

She didn't wish to marry him, but she wished to keep him. She wished to give him nothing, but that he should give her all. It is a bargain not unfrequently levied in love. (p. 776)

By a clever stylistic device, Thackeray has used the antithetical balance of the first two sentences quoted above, to convey the nature of their relationship over fifteen years. The irony of Amelia's attitude is surely underlined by the close of Chapter 66; after Georgy has suffered the anguish of seeing Dobbin go, we are assured that everyone loves the Colonel. The author observes: 'As for Emmy, had she not done her duty? She had her picture of George for a consolation' (p. 779).

It is Becky who really has the last word. Her constant praise of Dobbin makes her popular with everybody, but of course she is playing her own game with Jos. Becky is, however, sensitive to the pests who annoy Amelia at Ostend, and won't let either of them be alone with her. She continues, to the very end, to be a developing character: her description of George Osborne is, after all, a succinct summary of all that we, the readers, have felt about him. Becky sympathetically kisses Amelia after her revelation about George, but reverts sharply to normality with shrieks of laughter on hearing that Amelia has already written to Dobbin. Thackeray's sentimental account of Dobbin and Amelia's reunion is tinged, rightly, with the sadness of a lost love that can never really be fulfilled. A compassionate irony plays over the final statement of the relationship: the words 'kind', 'gentle' and 'gratify' used to describe Dobbin's every action to Amelia, lack the one word, 'love', which had sustained him 'for every day and hour for eighteen years' (p. 792).

Characterization

However much we may be caught up – emotionally, intellectually or morally – in the adventures, crises and triumphs of characters in fiction, we must always remember that their lives only exist within that fiction. They are not *real* people in the sense that we are *real*. Their flesh and blood is, so to speak, the flesh and blood of the imagination, intellect and morality of their creator. They certainly possess realistic traits, otherwise we would not respond to them, but their lives are circumscribed by plot, action and ultimate finality. Characters live on in our imaginations, and if we read and re-read a novel, we sometimes find that our own initial preconceptions of them change. We might notice some subtlety, some nuance in presentation which we had not observed before, or find a complexity which makes a particular character fuller and more vivid to us. They approximate to what we know, or sense, or imagine.

Most great novels live through the presentation of their characters. When we have finished reading a novel – and indeed while we are reading – we find ourselves loving, hating, sympathizing with or disapproving of its characters. In fiction, character is fact; that is not a paradox, but a truth: we are caught up in the many adventures of Tom Jones; in the sufferings, anguished and drawn out, of Clarissa; in Elizabeth's battle with her own pride and prejudice, as well as Darcy's; in the passion of Heathcliff and Cathy. These brief references take us up to Thackeray's own time and *Vanity Fair*, which appeared in the same year as *Wuthering Heights*. In the work of Thackeray's great contemporary, Dickens, characters are sometimes endowed with a subtle psychological connotation, and sometimes they are compelling caricatures – brilliant, idiosyncratic and memorably distorted.

It is not until we read George Eliot, whose last work, *Daniel Deronda*, was published in 1876, that the emphasis on the psychological integration of character predominates. Dorothea Brooke and Gwendolen Harleth are presented with an immediacy of psychological motivation, and we share their sufferings. George Eliot's novels are a watershed; after her, Hardy and the great twentieth-century writers like Lawrence, Joyce and Virginia Woolf develop, extend and probe both the conscious and subconscious in their construction of character.

Thackeray's modes of characterization in *Vanity Fair* are a compound of physical description and particular psychological facets, rather than a full-scale integration. This presentation is frequently accompanied by commentary of a moral or ironic nature, so that we are *told* what characters do and at the same time given an authorial gloss on the event. This in no way diminishes the effect the characters have on us; indeed it sometimes enhances that effect, for Thackeray has a particular awareness of character in its immediate context, and a constant adherence to natural human reactions and interactions. Admittedly, there is a tendency towards caricature, but this is sometimes misleading; Thackeray himself is partly responsible for this ambiguity by his reference to the 'Manager of the Performance' and 'puppets' – both indicating a lack of depth in presentation.

It would be wrong and inaccurate to see Thackeray as a presenter of flat characters, for his major figures – and some minor ones – develop over the course of the narrative, just as people develop over the course of life. Note the progressive changes in Rawdon Crawley, the sudden onset of spirit in Amelia and Lady Jane, and the movement of compassion – or something like it – in old Osborne at the very end. Indeed, some characters who appear to be caricatures, for example Peggy O'Dowd, exhibit not merely recognizable traits but convincingly human ones. This is one of Thackeray's major achievements; he can coin a character, apparently freshly minted from the imagination, who quickly passes out of the narrative but is a marked individual while he is in it, like Steyne, his hireling Wenham, or Jim Crawley. Moreover Thackeray's caricatures, like those of Dickens, are often memorable, such as General Tufto, the Bareacres and, above all, the 'reeling old Silenus' Sir Pitt Crawley.

In his presentation of character Thackeray is subtle, ironic and broadly humanitarian, but with a scathing satirical edge which relentlessly castigates moral obloquy and pretentious social advancement. While all his characters are being given names and environments, we are simultaneously aware of the author's approval or disapproval of their actions and motives. Yet as we shall see, the author's opinion at any given moment does not militate against their vibrant and convincing individualities. Indeed, because of Thackeray's unerring sense of perspective, it frequently enhances the quality of our own appraisal.

Rebecca Sharp

In his preface to *Vanity Fair*, which he entitled 'Before the Curtain', Thackeray refers to the fact that 'The famous little Becky Puppet has been pronounced to be uncommonly flexible in the joints, and lively on the wire' (p. 34). It is a modest distancing from his achievement in creating the most impressive and vital (if unpleasant) character in his novel and, arguably, in nineteenth-century fiction. In the 'Novel Without a Hero' Becky is something of an anti-heroine, and her 'flexibility' – her resilience, opportunism, capacity for intrigue and quintessential egoism – make her the microcosmic centre of *Vanity Fair*. The subtlety of her presentation shows the depth at which Thackeray worked, for Becky's character is developed in terms of nature and nurture – the child is recognizably mother of the woman.

The young Becky, deprived of status at Chiswick Mall, has a temper, illustrated by her throwing back Johnson's Dictionary and her 'blasphemy' in praise of France and Bonaparte (p. 47). Thackeray 'explains' her; and although the picture is of someone who has never done a good action to anyone, a close reading of the summary of her early life provides us with some sympathetic insight, and explains the chip-on-the-shoulder attitude which characterizes the young Becky. She had 'the dismal precocity of poverty' and 'she never had been a girl, she said; she had been a woman since she was eight years old' (p. 29). Her precocity is sexual as well as social, and prior to her arrival at Miss Pinkerton's she had enjoyed the company of men, her acting and mimicry – two qualities which remain with her – being much in evidence. In fact Becky is an actress throughout, a professional in a world of society amateurs.

The main reasons for Becky's success lie in her ability to make appearance reality for those who succumb to her charm. Her roles range from loving mother (she *hates* her child) to sentimental piety (evident in her counterfeit interest in Lady Southdown's tracts, and her good works at the end of the novel in Bath and Cheltenham). From the outset Becky envies those who have had a better start in life (like Miss Swartz), and sets out to acquire those accomplishments which will serve her purpose of self-advancement. Her genuine independence is shown early, when she stands up to and outfaces Miss Pinkerton.

Thackeray transforms Becky rapidly; she is pale but he stresses her eyes, and soon after her introduction to Russell Square and Queen's Crawley we are made aware of her physicality. Becky is conveyed as sexually attractive in figure, features and manner; few women, apart from Amelia, like her, although some respond to her flattery. She always has an eye to the main chance – the cashmere shawls Jos gives to his sister show her at once that here is the chance of a profitable conquest. But Becky at Russell Square is, so to speak, a manipulator in training; her inveigling of Jos is a necessary apprenticeship. Because of the ironic authorial tone we are not entirely out of sympathy with her aims; as the narrator points out, 'Miss Sharp had no kind parent to arrange these delicate matters for her' (p. 57). The real mark of Becky's independence is that she has always had to fend for herself. Her vivid imagination carries her forward to possibilities, and her ignorance at this stage (witness the chili episode) is to be transformed into a determined acquisition of knowledge and useful experience. She ingratiates herself with the servants, flatters Jos, hints at her pathetic future ('I'll do it when – when I'm gone' (p. 69)) and sings an enchanting song, her green eyes binding Jos in 'a web of green silk' (p. 76). But the bowl of rack punch at Vauxhall undoes her.

Becky's adaptability is immediately evident when she meets Sir Pitt. She cross-questions Mrs Tinker, writes a vivacious and entertaining letter to Amelia from Queen's Crawley ('Rebecca is a droll funny creature, to be sure' (p. 116) asserts Thackeray in extenuation, or perhaps delight at his own creation, as this character develops) and before a year has passed she has conquered Sir Pitt. Her second letter to Amelia is an index to her advance. It is clear-sighted as well as satirical and a comparison with the first letter shows a new sophistication, almost as if Becky has mastered the art of expression and gained assurance and confidence. She sees into and through all those around her, and there are delightful hints of a liaison with Rawdon. Becky has learnt discretion and a deepening cunning; she now has several strings to her bow – Miss Crawley, Rawdon and old Sir Pitt – and, gambler that she is, invests her talents in the hope that at least one will yield the dividend of social advancement and riches. I use the latter term deliberately, for Becky is acquisitive – the basic criterion for success in Vanity Fair – and always at the expense of others.

She plays Rawdon off against Miss Crawley, knowing that the longer she keeps him at a distance the more secure he will be ultimately. Yet Becky, for all her cleverness and social skill, can be guilty of error, perhaps because she keeps too many things going at the same time. She watches over Miss Crawley's sick bed, effectively ousts Briggs, extends her repertoire to a fine imitation of that poor woman, but misreads the Radical assertions of Miss Crawley, finding them conservative when it comes to Becky's marriage. Thackeray, wishing to stress the unscrupulousness of Becky's attendance on the old lady, removes her from the reader's sympathy by using her surname, an effective distancing:

Sharp watched this graceless bedside with indomitable patience. Nothing escaped her; and, like a prudent steward, she found a use for everything ... she was never out of temper; always alert; she slept light, having a perfectly clear conscience ... (p. 173)

But, in a sense, this devotion causes other aspects to escape her. She gambles for marriage, wins Rawdon but loses Sir Pitt (and what wouldn't she have given to be Lady Crawley!) and Miss Crawley.

Even before these intrigues she demonstrates her assurance in a patronizing acidity to George Osborne, discomfiting that arrogant young officer by giving him 'a little nod, so cool and killing' (p. 181) and telling him (how far it is from the truth, but how hurtful to this upstart from a commercial family), 'what a difference eighteen months' experience makes! – eighteen months spent, pardon me for saying so, with gentlemen' (p. 182). Becky is never at a loss for jibes, and also tells George (ironically, considering her own background), 'You can't help your pedigree' (p. 182). She does, as Thackeray tells us, lose her presence of mind when Sir Pitt proposes, and 'wept some of the most genuine tears that ever fell from her eyes' (p. 186).

Becky turns Sir Pitt's proposal to advantage with Miss Crawley, who is still ignorant of her marriage to Rawdon, and demurely admits to another attachment. Romance and sentiment are the stuff of Vanity Fair, and in playing this card Becky is calculating on Miss Crawley relenting. The affecting letter she writes to Miss Briggs – a cunning move to get that lady, whom she displaced, on her side by choosing to confide in her – has unfortunate repercussions. This is not only because of her misreading of Miss Crawley; what Becky could not know was that the arrival of Mrs Bute would effectively supplant her in her practical capacity. Becky's faith in herself, however, is unaffected. Rawdon doubts that his aunt will relent, but Becky asserts, '*I'll* make your fortune', and Thackeray observes that 'Delilah patted Samson's cheek' (p. 204). This is one of the many appropriate references to the match, and the italicized '*I'll*' emphasizes the fact that anyway Becky will make *her* fortune. She does, and loses it, ruining most of the people with whom she comes into contact in the process.

'What an artful little woman!' says Becky of Mrs Bute (p. 210), and the description fits herself more adequately than her earlier 'I'm no angel' (p. 47), which fails to convey either her flexibility or her liveliness 'on the wire'. She adapts to modest married life still hoping that Miss Crawley will come round, expresses sorrow at Mr Sedley's failure and begins to be admired for her sexual attractiveness – perfectly summarized by Squills (p. 235). Her acting always partakes of the melodramatic and when she and Rawdon pass Miss Crawley out driving we are told that, 'she clasped her hands, and looked towards the spinster with a face of agonized attachment and devotion' (p. 236). If this is overacting, her reception of George Osborne in Brighton is consummate: 'I thought you seemed careless about dear Amelia. It was that made me angry' (p. 264), while her honesty about their duns and creditors shows just how calculating she is.

She sums up Dobbin – and his secret – accurately, but sets out to ensnare George, General Tufto and anyone within her orbit who is either attractive or useful – generally the latter. The extent of Becky's sexual attraction is given considered weight by the author before the catalogue of her successes:

> She had put on the neatest and freshest white frock imaginable, and with bare shoulders and a little necklace, and a light blue sash, she looked the image of youthful innocence and girlish happiness. (p. 290)

She outshines Amelia, makes up to George, imagines an 'aquatic meeting' of reconciliation with Miss Crawley, interrogates Briggs when she 'accidentally' meets her, writes on Rawdon's behalf to his aunt and roars with laughter when Rawdon only succeeds in getting twenty pounds out of the old lady.

Becky in Brussels is in her natural element; she plays Tufto off against George, delighting in their mutual jealousy, and creates a 'brilliant apparition' (p. 338) at the Opera. She is the centre of attraction at the Duchess of Richmond's ball, patronizes and criticizes Amelia, monopolizes George and receives his note ('She had been used to deal with notes in early life' (p. 343)). Brought face to face with the reality of war, Becky's shrewdness ensures that if Rawdon dies she will be tolerably provided for. When the regiment leaves 'she put her bouquet of the ball into a glass of water, and went to bed and slept very comfortably' (p. 352). Next day she reckons up her assets and determines to visit Amelia. Thackeray's evaluation of his creature is laconic and strikingly interesting:

> If this is a novel without a hero, at least let us lay claim to a heroine. No man in the British army which has marched away, not the great Duke himself, could be more cool or collected in the presence of doubts and difficulties, than the indomitable little aide-de-camp's wife. (p. 353)

Despite the irony, this is an admission; just as Becky has taken over the reader, so she has conquered her creator. The tone cannot hide the infinite vitality of her presentation.

With the battle of Waterloo imminent Becky, having flattered Jos (and accused him of being false to her in the past), now visits Amelia, and, realizing the justice of Amelia's accusations, is 'touched in spite of herself' (p. 366). She shifts her ground, telling Jos as she goes that Amelia 'is very unwell' (p. 367). Thackeray asserts that Becky was 'of a good-natured and obliging disposition' (p. 367), and finds Amelia's words a compliment to her own triumph with George. She even finds time to laugh at Peggy O'Dowd's sincerity – which she finds grotesque – and then humiliates the Bareacres family, who in the past have snubbed her. The resilience and courage which we have noted in Becky's past are here allied to a mean commercial streak and a superb assumption of social superiority over

'The infuriate Countess' (p. 376). She decides to sell her horses at an extortionate price to Jos and, as the flight continues, Becky calculates that there is nothing to lose by staying; she stitches her trinkets and banknotes about her body and considers that Rawdon 'is worth ten of this creature' (p. 383), meaning George.

With Waterloo over Becky lays siege to Miss Crawley, sending her fake mementoes of the battle, and spends a comfortable winter in Paris. Her chameleon personality easily adapts to society, into which she has gained an entrée by using Miss Crawley's name. Her child is born on 26 March 1816, she and Rawdon stay in Paris for two or three years and then Becky, whose nature could certainly be described as restless, decides to push her husband's fortune – really, of course, her own – in England again. Little Rawdon, an irrelevance as far as she is concerned, is left on the continent and Becky, ever financially adroit, pays off her husband's creditors in England 'with fifteen hundred pounds of ready money, more than ten times the amount of debts' (p. 434). In fact her business acumen is such that she 'cons' Raggles into giving up his house to her (he is later bankrupted and imprisoned) and proceeds to continue to live on credit in England.

With Miss Crawley dead, Becky is instrumental in bringing Pitt back into her circle, which is dominated by Lord Steyne. She is fond of Rawdon but virtually ignores him and their son. Presented as sexually provocative, she decides to employ a 'sheep-dog' in the form of a companion who will guard her reputation, but who in effect will turn a blind eye to her intrigues. The death of old Sir Pitt invigorates Becky, for she anticipates a possible entrée into English society via the new Sir Pitt. She and Rawdon leave the watch-dog Briggs in charge while they go to Queen's Crawley for the funeral, Becky confident that this will give her an opportunity to influence the new Baronet. First she wins over Lady Jane by professing an interest in her children (sheer hypocrisy this) and then suffers 'Lady Macbeth's' tracts and medicine. She so ingratiates herself with the new Sir Pitt that he actually calls her Rebecca, and she occupies her days at Queen's Crawley by charming the other members of the family.

Becky has Sir Pitt to stay in Curzon Street; he is completely taken in by 'this artless little creature's hospitalities, so kindly were they pressed, so frankly and amiably offered' (p. 517), which indicates the convincing range of Becky's hypocrisy. She even cooks for him and affects to hem a shirt for her son, in an attempt to get money out of Sir Pitt. But Becky's good nature is tried by her innocent son, who listens outside the door to hear her sing, and she boxes his ears. She hates little Rawdon, who symbolizes motherhood, and marriage – factors which interfere with her ambition to gain access to society through Lord Steyne and Sir Pitt.

Thackeray says that she is 'guiltless very likely' but 'she was writhing and pushing onward towards what they call "a position in society"' (p. 523). Hence the cultivation of Sir Pitt is essential, and she is intelligent enough to read his pamphlet on Malt and to imply that he is more widely known and respected than in fact he is. Every now and then she overdoes things, as when she calls little Rawdon to her and kisses him before everyone else, eliciting the response 'You never kiss me at home, mamma' (p. 530). Her behaviour repeats itself: just as she lured George Osborne from Amelia so she lures Sir Pitt from Lady Jane, though here without any sexual suggestions. She sneers at Lady Jane and regards her with baleful eyes, for the simple fact is that Becky dislikes virtue and homely domesticity; as Thackeray puts it, 'she spurned children and children-lovers' (p. 534).

Becky's presentation at Court is the highlight of her career, and the commentary which accompanies it does much to explain her motivation and to give a consistency to her character which is later seen in her good works. Thackeray observes, 'so to be, and to be thought, a respectable woman, was Becky's aim in life, and she got up the genteel with amazing assiduity, readiness, and success' (p. 556). Her jewels are supplied by Steyne and Sir Pitt (unbeknown to Rawdon and Lady Jane). The effect of the presentation is that Becky extends her range yet again; she becomes a loyalist, talks virtuously and cuts those of her previous acquaintance whom she considers disreputable. She exemplifies all the vanities of the Fair for, in due course, she is to be treated in the same way by others. In fact she endures snubs at Steyne's dinner, but still manages to move his wife to tears by the quality of her singing.

Yet Becky's movements in society reflect that restlessness to which we have already referred, and there are moments when we feel she might have taken another course (as she herself temporarily considered on her second visit to Queen's Crawley). For in the great world of society she is bored, and there are times when she thinks, 'I wish I were out of it ... I would rather be a parson's wife, and teach a Sunday School than this' – and, best of all, and most appropriate to Thackeray's conception of himself as 'manager' – 'O how much gayer it would be to wear spangles and trousers, and dance before a booth at a fair' (p. 587). The irony of this is superb, for not only is Becky dancing at a booth of the biggest fair of all, she is also remembering her cosmopolitan roots. This is Thackeray's way of integrating his character; Becky is presented consistently from beginning to end.

She flatters everyone she meets by her politeness, concern, charm and simulated humility. Sometimes she routs her opponents by a 'knack of adopting a demure *ingenue* air, under which she was most dangerous'

(p. 590). Her acting range in life is reflected by her range in performance; she is aptly cast as Clytemnestra in the first charade at Gaunt House, and later perhaps even more appropriately as Philomèle, for she is acclaimed as 'the NIGHTINGALE of the evening' (p. 599). The ambiguity (nightingale is slang for prostitute, and was first used in the 1840s) is part of Thackeray's irony as his little Becky reaches the top of the social ladder when she is morally lowest. Such is the acclaim for her performances that Becky, usually calculating and able to laugh at herself, is carried away:

> Little Becky's soul swelled with pride and delight at these honours; she saw fortune, fame, fashion before her. Lord Steyne was her slave; followed her everywhere, and scarcely spoke to any one in the room beside; and paid her the most marked compliments and attention. (p. 600)

She never again reaches those ephemeral heights.

After this Becky's descent begins. She is a bad and callous mother, and when little Rawdon goes to school she treats her husband with contempt, and allows Steyne to provide for Briggs in order to get that worthy woman out of their way. Becky has, of course, ruined Briggs financially anyway, but now her acting takes on a cruel streak. Accomplished liar as she is, she tells Steyne that Rawdon has treated her savagely and makes up to her husband after Briggs has been paid off by Steyne. Becky meanwhile tells Sir Pitt that she will do anything he commands to maintain the family's reputation, and yet lets Steyne come and go freely. Becky is besotted with what she thinks is her position in society. Once again she is deluded. Disowned by Sir Pitt after the charades, she encounters the obstinacy of Rawdon, who spends all his time with her, thus forestalling Steyne.

The nature of Becky's ambition, lust and hypocrisy is finely conveyed by Thackeray at the end of Chapter 52:

> 'Let us always go on so, dear Rawdon. How nice it would be, and how happy we should always be, if we had but the money!' He fell asleep after dinner in his chair; he did not see the face opposite to him, haggard, weary, and terrible; it lighted up with fresh candid smiles when he woke. It kissed him gaily. He wondered that he had ever had suspicions. (pp. 612–13)

Becky's letter to her 'poor old monster' (p. 617) is a masterpiece of dissembling cunning, even down to the headache and heartache which she affects to have. But it also marks her moral depths. Although Becky promises to borrow money from Steyne to free Rawdon, there is little doubt that she conspired with Steyne to have him arrested by the bailiffs. The confrontation between Rawdon and Steyne – the highest dramatic moment of *Vanity Fair* – finds Becky for once in a subordinate role. She pleads her innocence, in fear of her 'strong, brave, and victorious' husband (p. 620), but without conviction. After Rawdon has gone, and certain that she is ruined, Becky considers suicide.

Thackeray's comment on his character is inlaid with a determination to keep up narrative tension and speculation. In effect, his questions are rhetorical:

> What *had* happened? Was she guilty or not? She said not; but who could tell what was the truth which came from those lips; or if that corrupt heart was in this case pure? All her lies and her schemes, all her selfishness and her wiles, all her wit and genius had come to this bankruptcy. (p. 622)

But Becky rallies, making the most of 'the uses of adversity'. She goes to Sir Pitt, tells him of Rawdon's appointment to Coventry Island ('It was intended as a surprise for him' (p. 637)), passionately kisses his hand and, condemned by Lady Jane, has the inward audacity to be rather pleased by the scene, attributing it to Lady Jane's jealousy.

Becky moves to Boulogne, and we do not meet her again until she turns up in Pumpernickel and makes her second, and successful play for Jos. Before that there is a retrospective chapter on her recent career which, although Thackeray claims he will deal with briefly, obviously has its own fascinations for him as well as for us. Again a close reading is essential to get the full picture of Becky. Thackeray casually remarks:

> And I am inclined to think that there was a period in Mrs Becky's life, when she was seized, not by remorse, but by a kind of despair, and absolutely neglected her person, and did not even care for her reputation. (pp. 738–9)

But those qualities of resilience, resolution and opportunism, which we have seen in her so often, resurface quickly.

When little Rawdon is made heir of Queen's Crawley, Becky writes him a 'most affectionate composition' (p. 740). Settled in Boulogne, she impresses her acquaintances by 'talking that easy, fashionable slipslop, which has so much effect upon certain folks of small breeding' (p. 741). But she is snubbed by those who courted her, and thinks with regret of her husband and how he would have protected her. She rouges and drinks, is forced to leave her lodgings, but becomes infinitely respectable, employing a kind of masochistic guise:

> She saw people avoiding her, and still laboriously smiled upon them; you never could suppose from her countenance what pangs of humiliation she might be enduring inwardly. (p. 743)

She builds up circles of people, but they are destroyed, so that she moves from place to place yet is always found out – 'pecked out of the cage by the real daws' (p. 744).

In any case, that restless spirit soon tires of respectability; Becky loves society, and 'could no more exist without it than an opium-eater without his dram' (p. 745). She returns to Brussels, makes a sketch of George Osborne's monument, and says of Amelia and the Sedleys, 'They were kind simple people' (p. 746). The next phase is her 'taste for disrespectability' (p. 747); in Rome she gives music lessons, consorts with disreputable officers, and is warned to leave the city by a factotum of Steyne's. Pumpernickel is admirably appropriate for her final phase of Bohemian existence. As Thackeray puts it, 'Becky had found a little nest – as dirty a little refuge as ever beauty lay hid in' (p. 755). Truly she is wearing spangles and trousers and dancing at the fair. Her entertainment of Jos is full of 'tender interest' (p. 756), but she has lost none of her animation. Her flattery, accompanied by a nostalgic falsification of their past, moves Jos and appears to move Becky, so that she buries 'her face for a moment on the bed' (p. 757), thus grotesquely clinking the hidden brandy bottle against a plate of cold sausage. When he is gone she follows her usual practice of mimicking him to the students with whom she lives.

The 'hardened little reprobate' (p. 763) is touched by Amelia's kindness, but she is almost caught out by questions about little Rawdon, forgetting his age and inventing lies about her own sufferings from 'a brain fever' (p. 763). With fresh opportunity at hand in the form of Jos, Becky's inventiveness reaches new heights, and she tells Amelia that Rawdon made her sacrifice 'her own fair fame so that he might procure advancement through the means of a very great and powerful but unprincipled man – the Marquis of Steyne' (p. 764). We further learn by eavesdropping on the students that Becky's voice has cracked. With Dobbin intent on winning Amelia away from her, Becky assumes the expression of a martyr. But her acting days are over, for she is now virtually certain of Jos, and she cleverly praises Dobbin to Amelia, knowing that if they marry she will be free to carry through her plans about Jos.

She gets Jos's portrait from Leipsic, moves to Ostend with Amelia and young George, but never lets her disreputable companions be alone with Amelia. In a remarkable tirade she damns the memory of George Osborne, sparing Amelia none of the details of that worthless man's infatuation for her, even producing the note George had written to her urging her to run away with him on the eve of Waterloo. She tells Amelia that she needs a husband to protect her, and when Amelia breaks down, 'the other soothed and kissed her – a rare mark of sympathy with Mrs Becky. She treated Emmy like a child, and patted her head' (p. 790). Becky proves to have some generosity of spirit here, a neat balancing of her selfishness with a capacity to respond to the needs of the moment.

We do not see Becky again, but her after-career as 'Lady Crawley' in Bath and Cheltenham is carefully catalogued. She has been left comfortably off by Jos's life insurance, which she obviously coerced that sad man to effect and which causes a scandal. She achieves, it appears, the respectability which she had sometimes craved, forsaking Vanity Fair for 'stalls at Fancy Fairs' on behalf of, among others, 'The Destitute Orange-girl' (p. 797).

The salient features of Becky's character have been given in context above, but a little more must be said here. Although she symbolizes vice, corruption, selfishness, ambition and many more undesirable qualities, Becky is presented as recognizably human. At the beginning of this section I said that she is seen as the product of nature and nurture, and Thackeray's consistency in his presentation of her is remarkable. The movement from pale, sandy-haired girl, to society queen, to rouged boarding-house queen, to respectability – which perhaps ought to be in inverted commas – is never less than convincing. She compels interest, commands admiration, invites condemnation and yet *fascinates* the reader as much as she obviously fascinated her creator. For let there be no mistake, Becky is a tyrant but, for the most part, good-humoured and cunningly charming with it. Moments of humility and remorse are beyond her, but she has a courage and tenacity which mark out the born survivor in Vanity Fair and in life.

Amelia Osborne

At first sight Amelia appears to be the conventionally idealized Victorian heroine, though Thackeray twice repeats his own disclaimer of her status. The early Thackerayan tone – though tinged with omnipresent irony – hardly brings her to life, for she is 'a dear little creature' (p. 43) who cries over a dead canary-bird and cannot be spoken to roughly. This beginning is inauspicious, almost Dickensian, and the reader may fear that this might be another Little Nell translated into a rather different social context. Amelia is always set in contradistinction to Becky, as goodness against corruption, naïveté against duplicity and simplicity against deviousness. She is inevitably gentle, tender-hearted and trusting, so much so that she is cloying and boring as well. Fortunately, such is Thackeray's art that he makes Amelia human, and consequently she develops as a character, acquiring some spirit on occasions and an almost wilful wrong-headedness over the years. Her innocence is qualified by natural vanity, for she is pleased when a young officer remarks of her 'A dem fine gal, egad!' (p. 53), and yet she is clear-sighted about her brother's egocentric nature, although she refrains from extended criticism of him. Though young and inexperienced, she is something of a matchmaker, and does her best to further Becky's initial siege of Jos.

Her own attachment to George – and remember that she has been bred up to it – is romantic, sentimental and engagingly blind. When Jos writes that he is going away to Cheltenham, it is Amelia who is upset and cries on her friend's account. Amelia is born to be a martyr, just as Becky is born to act like one, and she suffers humiliation and snubbing at the hands of the Misses Osborne, particularly since George neglects her, and she worries when the regiment in which he serves is going to be sent abroad. The nature of her love, her obsession, is chronicled by the author with full contemporary exaggeration:

> The fate of Europe was Lieutenant George Osborne to her. His dangers being over, she sang Te Deum. He was her Europe: her emperor: her allied monarchs and august prince regent. He was her sun and moon; and I believe she thought the grand illumination and ball at the Mansion House, given to the sovereigns, were especially in honour of George Osborne. (p. 151)

The effect of this distortion is to reduce Amelia's effectiveness as a character in interaction with others. This is emphasized by the author's commentary when, for example, he tells us that 'her kind thoughts sped away as if they were angels and had wings, and flying down the river to Chatham and Rochester, strove to peep into the barracks where George was' (p. 158). It militates against realism, conditions us to take Amelia for what she is, a doll – or even a puppet. But there is method in Thackeray's management of Amelia; the purer she is, the more unworthy of her is George Osborne and the more malign is Becky's conduct. Until she meets Peggy O'Dowd she has no one in whom she can confide, and we remember the night when her father tells her mother that they are ruined. Amelia lies lonely and afraid, while 'Her heart tried to persist in asserting that George Osborne was worthy and faithful to her, though she knew otherwise' (p. 215). In fact George, his arm metaphorically twisted by Dobbin, marries her, but Amelia's insight here is to be proved true when, after that marriage, George pays more and more attention to Becky.

At one time, when her father forbids her to see George, she longs for death; Dobbin tells George that she is dying, and he goes to her. Restored to health she now believes that George is 'the greatest and best of men' (p. 238), though she affects to be jealous of her old friend Miss Swartz. At first Amelia likes Dobbin, but in a superficial way, and soon finds that she is troubled by George's attentions to Becky. She also ponders on her selfishness in marrying rather than staying to look after her parents.

She feels neglected after a week of marriage and a couple of days later visits her parents in Fulham, unaccompanied by George. There she re-experiences all her doubts about George but gains strength from prayer. When she joins the regiment Amelia enjoys the admiration of the officers and the warm friendship of Peggy O'Dowd, George of course being later ashamed of Amelia having to be in the company of 'damned vulgar women' (p. 327).

Amelia is happy in Brussels before the Crawleys arrive, but this soon gives way to moping and pining as she is socially eclipsed by the brilliant Becky. She stays awake on the fateful night of the ball, waiting for George's return, and is quite helpless in the morning as he packs to leave. Comforted by Pauline the cook, Amelia's spirit returns, and when Becky comes to visit her she behaves in a manner which is strangely at variance with all that she has done before:

> 'Why did you come between my love and me? Who sent you to separate those whom God joined, and take my darling's heart from me – my own husband? Do you think you could love him as I did? His love was everything to me. You knew it, and wanted to rob me of it. For shame, Rebecca; bad and wicked woman – false friend and false wife.' (p. 366)

It is a finely dramatic moment, but curiously lacking in realism. What follows – Amelia's forgetting Becky's presence, her smiling, her smoothing down George's pillow – shows a mind unhinged by what has happened. But it is not convincingly done, for there has been little or no preparation for it. With rumours of the battle arriving, Thackeray seeks to deepen the impression of Amelia's state – 'Her doubts and terrors had reached their paroxysm; and the poor girl, who for many hours had been plunged into stupor, raved and ran hither and thither in hysteric insanity – a piteous sight' (p. 379). She loses herself in attending to Stubble, and stays with Peggy O'Dowd while her brother urges her to leave.

Amelia is widowed and has a baby boy, but we are told that the doctors 'had feared for her life or for her brain' (p. 424). One wonders, indeed, if Thackeray's presentation of Amelia is meant to show that she did not fully recover from her dementia, hence her obsessional worship of the memory of George and of her child. She hardly notices Dobbin when he takes his leave of her, despite all his kindness. Even her quarrel with her mother seems to take on proportions as unnatural as her obsession with her child; and her conversations with little George show the depth at which Thackeray is working:

> ... into his ears she poured her sentimental secrets unreservedly, and into his only. The very joy of this woman was a sort of grief, or so tender, at least, that its expression was tears. Her sensibilities were so weak and tremulous, that perhaps they ought not to be talked about in a book. (p. 457)

The insight and the reticence alike help to make Amelia a fuller character, and we see her keeping 25 April and 18 June every year as consecrated days. It is not sentimental, but rather frightening, and her possession of the child more complex than it at first appears. Amelia's religion is the worship of the dead: 'And each time they prayed to God to bless dear papa, as if he were alive and in the room with them' (p. 461).

The subtlety of Thackeray's presentation is such that when Amelia hears that Dobbin is going to marry Glorvina she is very happy, so happy that 'by some impulse of which I cannot explain the meaning, she took George in her arms and kissed him with an extraordinary tenderness' (p. 466). It is an inspirational movement of character in action. The simple truth is that Amelia does not know herself, although when she writes to Dobbin we are told that 'the news of the marriage removed the reserve which she had kept up towards him' (p. 505). We note a consistency in her actions; just as she is deluded about George's real nature, so she misinterprets her own relationship to Dobbin. Even the underlined phrases in her letter to Dobbin are a psychological notation of her motives.

Amelia teaches Georgy all she can, is distressed when he gladly goes to school and thinks of herself as 'an old woman' (p. 538). She is bitterly resentful of old Osborne when he proposes to make her a decent allowance if she should marry again. Poverty and deprivation reduce her to parting with the fine shawl Dobbin had given her, in order to buy presents for Georgy. Faced by her angry mother, she realizes what she has done. There is no more moving account of the ambiguity of love in the whole of *Vanity Fair*:

She saw it all now. Her selfishness was sacrificing the boy. But for her he might have wealth, station, education, and his father's place, which the elder George had forfeited for her sake. She had but to speak the words, and her father was restored to competency: and the boy raised to fortune. (p. 544)

It is the beginning of self-recognition, but it doesn't alleviate her anguish. Over it all looms the author's irony, for if she sacrifices little George to the rich world of Vanity Fair he will be able to indulge those traits of selfishness which, we note already, he has inherited from his worthless father.

We have already commented on the superb brevity with which Amelia's sacrifice is conveyed. The pathos of her lonely walks to Russell Square, the 'little black profile' she has done of Georgy 'for a shilling' (p. 651) and her delight in the red morocco case he gives her, are Amelia's crumbs of comfort. She does all she can after her mother's death to give her father comfort too, is greatly moved by Dobbin's arrival and continues to idolize her son. Made aware of Dobbin's love for her by Polly, she speaks of him as a brother, and George as an angel, wondering whether she knows of anyone suitable for Dobbin to marry (she is of course relieved that he did not marry Glorvina). But gradually new insights come to her. She realizes that it was Dobbin who bought the old piano and not George. She receives his declaration of love but is seemingly dead to passion – 'George is my husband, here and in heaven' (p. 693). The change in her fortunes – the annuity left to her by old Osborne – finds Amelia susceptible, forgiving, but much happier than hitherto. She soon realizes that Dobbin has supported them in their adversity and prays for him with gratitude, but nothing more. As Thackeray puts it:

> If she thought of any other return, the image of George stood up out of the grave, and said, 'You are mine, and mine only, now and for ever.' (p. 709)

She considers society 'cruelly genteel' (p. 714) and goes on the foreign tour, finding time to sketch and to enjoy music for the first time in her life. She depends upon Dobbin in her everyday existence and begins to acquire genuine culture, arousing a great deal of attention when she responds with 'wonder and delight' (p. 722) to a performance of *Fidelio*. Her innocence is continually stressed, for she does not understand the sophistications of Vanity Fair, which consist of much bowing and simpering, particularly in Pumpernickel. Thackeray also stresses her soft disposition, preparing us for her reception of Becky by saying (of Amelia) that she 'was such a mean-spirited creature, that – we are obliged to confess it – she could even forget a mortal injury' (p. 759). At first Amelia asserts that she cannot see Becky but, moved by Jos's tale of her woes, she bursts out impetuously, 'let us go and see her this minute' (p. 762).

She is moved because she believes that little Rawdon has been taken by force from Becky, and naturally associates this with her own loss of Georgy to his grandfather. Ingenuous and gullible, she believes what Becky tells her of Rawdon, and continues to tyrannize Dobbin. When the latter objects to Becky coming to live with them she fiercely rebukes him, and communes with her 'saint in heaven' (p. 769) – the picture of George. Wrong-headed in her bitterness with Dobbin for daring to hint at the truth of George's affair with Becky, Amelia actually believes that her own jealousy of her 'friend' was groundless. When Dobbin comes to see her the next day we realize just how wilfully insensitive she has been to him. She is so moved with anger and emotion as she talks to him that her teeth are chattering, and she stands 'scared and silent' (p. 776) when Dobbin says 'Let it end' and 'I have spent enough of my life at this play' (p. 776).

Amelia finds that Becky has her uses, for she tells her in no uncertain terms how badly she (Amelia) has treated Dobbin. Amelia encourages her to talk of Dobbin, but initially sticks to her religious principles and loyalty to the memory of George. Gradually her mood changes, and we are told that when she looks at her husband's portrait 'perhaps she reproached it, now William was gone' (p. 781). She becomes peevish, pale and thin after her 'heroic sacrifice' (p. 781). Many times she impresses upon Georgy what they both owe to William, thus revealing obliquely the secrets of her own heart. The author's comment as Amelia breaks down shows his concern with character at the moment of self-revelation:

> Who shall analyse those tears and say whether they were sweet or bitter? Was she most grieved because the idol of her life was tumbled down and shivered at her feet, or indignant that her love had been so despised ... (p. 790)

Amelia herself answers the questions when she says 'I may love him with all my heart now' (p. 790), and she admits to Becky that she has already written to Dobbin.

Their reunion, which should be joyful, has Amelia looking up at Dobbin and seeing the reproach in his face. Thackeray ranges wide in his imagery of fulfilment, but nothing is more pathetic – and true – than his reference to Amelia as a 'tender little parasite' (p. 792). Half a lifetime has been wasted by Amelia's obduracy, and Thackeray's alternating treatment of her, from innocence to near-madness, to suffering and sacrifice, are in no way inconsistent. Amelia's blind loyalty and devotion to George, whom Becky superbly describes as 'that low-bred cockney dandy, that padded booby, who had neither wit, nor manners, nor heart' (p. 789), is as natural, unfortunate and tragic as our own illusions. Given her youth, poverty and deprivation, and considering the change from security to domestic adversity that Amelia suffers, she is a triumph of fictional characterization.

William Dobbin

Thackeray cherished a great affection for 'old Dob' and, despite his novel's subtitle, he created a hero vastly superior to conventional fictional heroes, who normally have good looks, intelligence, extraordinary physical prowess and success in love. Dobbin has only the second of these qualities, and finally the last, though it is only a qualified success, as he himself recognizes. His name and background at first militate against realism, but his naturally heroic qualities are soon in evidence in the fight with Cuff. Dobbin wins and, like Amelia later, devotes himself to the boy he has befriended – George Osborne. One wonders if Thackeray ever had second thoughts about the name: 'Dobbin' invites caricature, and indeed descriptions of his early appearance, clumsiness and general lack of social acceptability, seem to confirm this. But, in common with Amelia, a closer look reveals a developing character. He appears to advantage at Vauxhall, protecting the courting couples and at one stage preventing a scene. He falls in love with Amelia at first sight, but at supper realizes that he has been completely forgotten and, as on so many occasions later, effaces himself. He returns to the box where Jos is making a fool of himself over Becky, and immediately shows that his is a presence to be reckoned with, though George, with typical insensitivity, asks him where he has been.

The inference we draw about Dobbin is that just as he mastered everything at school after difficulty, so he has mastered his profession. He is endearing and kind without being cloying, serves George and Amelia, comforts the junior officers and has no time for any of the rakish activities which so many of his fellows enjoy. He is responsible and open, and the only implicit criticism against him is his unsullied devotion to Amelia, which leads to an interest in the young couple's affairs and brings him into conflict with both Mr Sedley and Mr Osborne.

He is sufficiently moved by George's neglect of Amelia to reveal their secret engagement to the rest of the officers. This action annoys George, who would have preferred to let that attachment remain a mystery. But Dobbin's questions get the better of him – 'Are you engaged?', 'Are you ashamed of it?' (p. 157). Dobbin lends, or rather gives, George money, buys the piano for Amelia without revealing he has done so and arranges the marriage – but not before he has lost his temper with his own sisters for suggesting that George 'could not marry a bankrupt's daughter' (p. 220). He realizes that the marriage had best take place quickly, and tries to get the broken Mr Sedley's consent. He fails, but is sustained by Amelia's obvious happiness with George, and acts as groomsman at the marriage. His reaction is painful:

Never since he was a boy had he felt so miserable and so lonely. He longed with a heart-sick yearning for the first few days to be over, that he might see her again. (p. 261)

Dobbin acts both as messenger and organizer: he brings news that the army is ordered to Belgium, and before that has tried to win over Mr Osborne. In doing so, he unfortunately encourages expectations in the breast of Jane Osborne. He tells her of the marriage, and then goes off to the City to see George's father. The argument is fierce but brief, and Dobbin's voice falters as he tells Osborne, 'You had best spare her, sir, for she's your son's wife' (p. 277). Again he has shown positive moral courage.

Dobbin is 'greatly respected in the regiment, as the best officer and the cleverest man in it' (p. 286), and upon learning of the imminent embarkation for France, attempts to restore young Stubble's morale. In Brighton he puts on a cheerful act for Amelia's sake, bears the brunt of George's anger at being disinherited, and, true to his own generous nature, tells George that 'I shall not forget my godson in my will' (p. 290). It is a brilliant ironic foreshadowing of the fact that he does not forget his godson in his life. Dobbin 'still kept up his character of rattle' (p. 295), but when Amelia joins the regiment and the officers all admire her, Dobbin loves hearing young Stubble talk about her. He also watches over her, and over George, before the embarkation, and even procures a Belgian servant for Jos. In Brussels, Dobbin preserves his distance from the rakish and fashionable entourage ('The nods between Rawdon and Dobbin were of the very faintest specimens of politeness' (p. 334)), confirms his opinion that Becky is a 'humbug' (p. 338) and is grateful for the forthrightness of Peggy O'Dowd. He sees less of George, who now consorts with the Crawleys, but brings the news that battle with the French is now imminent. He sees Amelia as she watches George pack, and she is so pale that her face 'haunted him afterwards like a crime' (p. 355). Even in action his thoughts are of Amelia, and we note that he carried Ensign Stubble, though wounded himself, in his arms. By a terrible irony he sends, via Stubble, the news that George is safe.

His intercession on Amelia's behalf with Mr Osborne is unsuccessful. After the birth of little George Dobbin continues to devote himself to Amelia, but he sees – and this is one of the most convincing aspects of his character – all that Amelia feels, realizing that there is no place for him in her heart. He visits Mr Sedley, who thinks that Dobbin is making away with George's money, and through his stammering and blushing says that he and his friends had paid George's debts. Dobbin's actions transcend the pettiness of Vanity Fair:

> William Dobbin had told a great falsehood to the old gentleman; having himself given every shilling of the money, having buried his friend, and paid all the fees and charges incident upon the calamity and removal of Amelia. (p. 463)

And of course he continues to support her from afar, 'always thinking about Amelia and her little boy' (p. 465).

One of Dobbin's most endearing qualities – even though it has only a passing importance in the narrative – is his resistance to the advances of Glorvina O'Dowd. Teased by his fellow officers, he remains in a 'state of the most odious tranquillity' (p. 509), considering himself 'too battered and old for such a fine young lady' (p. 509). He is sickened by Amelia's apparent blessing of his supposed marriage and peruses all the letters she has written to him – 'how cold, how kind, how hopeless, how selfish they were!' (p. 512) – thus uncovering in his honesty the paradox of Amelia.

Dobbin reappears after a long absence, when Georgy has been made a gentleman. He has learned from Jos, who travelled home with him, that Amelia is not married, and his spirits quickly rise. On arrival at Southampton he wishes to go immediately to London, dresses carefully and is taken by Polly to see Amelia sitting with old Sedley. There follows one of those many moments which could have changed the course of the novel:

He took the two little hands between his two, and held them there. He was speechless for a moment. Why did he not take her in his arms, and swear that he would never leave her? She must have yielded: she could not but have obeyed him. (p. 678)

Domestic proximity to Amelia brings only partial bliss: her praise of her child, likening him to the father, causes Dobbin deep suffering – a suffering exacerbated by Amelia's delusion that it was George who had bought her the old piano. It precipitates her recognition and his proposal, but he cannot penetrate Amelia's obduracy or idolatry and has to be content with friendship. He is much admired by little George however, and the author defines the Major's qualities which command respect – 'simplicity ... good humour ... various learning quietly imparted ... general love of truth and justice' (p. 695). Even old Osborne is moved to shake hands with Dobbin and call him 'an honest feller' (p. 705), and is moved again when Dobbin, ever eloquent on the subject of Amelia, tells him of the widow's sufferings. Old Osborne relents and remembers Dobbin in his will in recognition of his 'kindness and bounty' (p. 709), as well as leaving him sufficient money to purchase the rank of Lieutenant-Colonel.

Dobbin uses the continental trip to further Amelia's social and cultural pleasures, seeking to make up for her years of deprivation, without mentioning his own. It is a tribute to the effect he has on people and his inherent generosity of spirit and breeding – I use the word deliberately in view of the upstarts in Vanity Fair – that he is liked, almost loved, by everybody. Becky recognizes his quality, so completely divorced from anything she has known, although she is also aware that he knows she is up to her old tricks. Dobbin overhears the students' conversation about Becky and he thinks back to George's intrigue with her, when he 'was too much hurt and ashamed to fathom that disgraceful mystery' (p. 767), about which he has always remained silent.

He is clear-sighted enough to see that Becky brings mischief with her, and objects to her being in the house, bringing down Amelia's wrath upon himself as a result. He uses all his persuasive powers to exclude Becky, but his sincerity and straightforwardness – he is not, says Thackeray, 'dexterous' – ensure his failure. His final words to Amelia show the quality, the endurance and devotion of the man, and the terrible self-knowledge which has finally come to him – 'No, you are not worthy of the love which I have devoted to you' (p. 776). He is right, but there is sadness in this recognition, not bitterness. Perhaps the greatest measure of the love he ought to have received is registered in young George's 'howling' after Dobbin has left. It is an ironic and unforced comment on his own mother's blindness.

Away from Amelia, he ponders with realistic resignation the years of his self-delusion, looking towards a future with a half-ironic humour, as he sees himself going into harness again, listening to the repetitive stories in the mess, living on half-pay and being scolded by his sisters. The author is identified with his character to such an extent in these final stages of the novel, that one is tempted to think of Thackeray's own wasted love for Jane Brookfield. Dobbin in positive adversity is more alive than Dobbin quietly serving George, Amelia and their son. We have already referred to the parasitic imagery in the final description of Amelia at their reunion; the imagery used to describe Dobbin's 'success' is that of romance and cheap sentiment, rather than reality. It is definitive of the nature of his illusions:

> The vessel is in port. He has got the prize he has been trying for all his life. The bird has come in at last. There it is with its head on his shoulder, billing and cooing close up to his heart, with soft outstretched fluttering wings. This is what he has asked for every day and hour for eighteen years. (p. 792)

The choice of words in the above quotation is precise and considered. Amelia is described in terms of an object or 'prize', indicating something gained but, by implication, much more lost. We understand his idealization of his daughter, his immersion in the 'History of the Punjaub' and his kindness and service to Amelia in the maturity of their lives. Dobbin, like so many of Thackeray's characters, moves from ostensible caricature to fully realized fictional personality. Thackeray is essentially a trans-forming novelist; the characters develop in his hands (he would diminish this by saying that he merely pulled the strings), for his sense of realism is such that he endows them at best with the complexity of life, at worst with recognizable traits which beg fuller investigation.

George Osborne

George Osborne, like Becky, epitomizes Vanity Fair. Handsome, selfish and irresponsible, he has a sense of social superiority and dandified ill-breeding, which makes him essentially an unsympathetic character. We know from his letters that Thackeray loathed him, and there is certainly a strong feeling in the reader that, despite all her sufferings, it is a good thing for Amelia that he didn't survive Waterloo. Even as a boy – and with what striking consistency Thackeray shows George's likeness to his son – we observe a feeling of superiority which makes him ashamed to acknowledge Dobbin as his champion against Cuff. Until, that is, Dobbin is winning and Cuff in the end proves himself a sportsman, thus ensuring that George will not suffer by his champion's victory. He patronizes Dobbin and receives devotion, friendship and sometimes money in return. As a boy George is spoilt by his mother, though often beaten by his father; this perhaps explains his vicious argument with old Osborne when he is urged to abandon Amelia and marry Miss Swartz, whom he calls the 'Hottentot Venus'. His description of the latter further indicates his snobbery and prejudice. At school he learns to ape those who are supposedly gentlemen and is encouraged by his father, who adopts the spurious Osborne coat of arms.

Engaged to Amelia from an early age, he accepts her adoration sometimes with warmth, though he rarely displays this, and often with condescension. His selfishness is such that he cannot accept that he is responsible when anything goes wrong, and his favourite recourse is to blame Dobbin – for example when he realizes that his father has virtually disinherited him. His redeeming features are sparse. He is sentimental, so that when Amelia returns all his letters and gifts he is moved to a kind of remorse. He takes Dobbin's advice – over gambling, for instance – but is rarely able to keep to it. He has a core of conscience, which makes him return to Amelia after the ball when he learns that the regiment's departure is imminent; but even here he is glad to be away the next morning, looking up at Amelia as he leaves, conscious as ever of his own image. Much later, Dobbin reveals George's repentance for what he has done to Amelia:

> 'I have been mixing in a foolish intrigue with a woman,' George said. 'I am glad we were marched away. If I drop, I hope Emmy will never know of that business. I wish to God it had never begun!' (p. 767)

It is a mark of consistency in his character that George should feel this way. In this instance, though, death supervenes before he can undo his good intentions.

George's gambling and neglect of Amelia are two major moral lapses – I am assuming that his entrenched egoism will be obvious to every reader – but we must also consider his social climbing and patronizing attitude towards those he considers his social inferiors. He meets his match in

Becky, who quickly graduates from the easily disparaged 'little Miss Sharp' to being the wife of Rawdon Crawley. Becky can not only put down this 'cockney dandy', but can also intrigue with him while keeping General Tufto within her power, and encouraging her husband to fleece George. The latter's acute sense of social position, his need for company and play, makes him ashamed of his marriage before many days have passed. His partial reform, when he takes Amelia with him to Brussels and pays her natural attention, is soon forgotten when Becky and the Tufto entourage appear.

It is not only intrigue that attracts George; he is the personification of that eternal snob, the name-dropper. This of course delights his like-minded father, who, however, pretends to despise it. Their quarrel is one of the highlights of the novel and, to be fair, George shows commendable spirit. He reveals, too, a true appreciation of the young and unspoiled Amelia:

> 'It's a shame, by heavens ... to play at fast and loose with a young girl's affections – and with such an angel as that – one so superior to the people amongst whom she lived, that she might have excited envy, only she was so good and gentle, that it's a wonder anybody dared to hate her. If I desert her, sir, do you suppose that she forgets me?' (p. 256)

This, like the letter which Sir William Dobbin delivers to George's father, constitutes a small core of goodness in a character who has already succumbed to the lures of Vanity Fair, and is merely a cypher for its corruption. The quotation illustrates another aspect of George – his impetuosity – which ranges from buying himself a diamond shirt-pin when he might have spent the money on Amelia, his gambling, his sudden determination to marry the day after the scene mentioned above, and his note to Becky, hidden in her bouquet at the Duchess of Richmond's ball.

George is not caricature; he is a dangerous egoist, akin to the superb Beatrix Esmond, and closer than he knows to Becky Sharp, whom he despises at first and is infatuated with later. He is human in interaction with Dobbin, romantic and ostentatious with Amelia and always aware of how he appears to others. An opportunist who moves up in society at the expense of his own and others' money, George is only occasionally brought back to a sense of reality and responsibility through the agency of his friend Dobbin.

Rawdon Crawley

There is only one greater triumph of characterization in *Vanity Fair* than Rawdon, and that is of course his wife, Becky. Rawdon is the supreme instance of the character who appears set in his ways of petty corruption, and then rises to something approaching nobility of character by finding integrity where we thought he had none. That the transformation is done convincingly is further evidence of Thackeray working in depth upon his characters. We hear interesting but morally damning things of Rawdon before we meet him. When he is sent down from Cambridge, his aunt purchases him a commission in the Life Guards Green Rawdon indulges in the fashionable sports and gambles immoderately, eventually fighting 'three bloody duels, in which he gave ample proofs of his contempt for death' (p. 131). He naturally employs the slang of the period in which to express his admiration of Becky – 'By Jove, she's a neat little filly!' (p. 138) – having no conception then of how she will emasculate and finally desecrate his character. But in these early days it is all romance for the 'heavy young dragoon' (p. 145), and Thackeray's ironic tone gives no hint of the development to come.

There is little doubt that Rawdon tries to make Becky his mistress, but is outmanoeuvred by that cunning 'little filly'. Rawdon is foolish in other ways; for example, he confides his love for Becky to Mrs Bute, and that black-eyed little agitator adroitly encourages the match, knowing that it can only rebound in her own favour. She also spurs Rawdon on to a positive proposal by implying that Sir Pitt is interested in Becky, which indeed he is. The 'mustachio-twiddler' becomes 'The Crawley heavy cavalry' (p. 175) and yet is utterly 'routed' by Becky. He seeks Becky's company increasingly as time passes, and is infatuated by her meretricious abilities, including her humiliation of that 'young flat', George Osborne (p. 178). Rawdon gives George 'a look of peculiar gratitude' (p. 183) when he presumes to warn him about Becky.

The extent of Rawdon's love for Becky – and it is love – is delightfully and ironically conveyed by Thackeray. 'Her words were oracles to him, her smallest actions marked by an infallible grace and wisdom' (p. 196), and Rawdon's own valuation is marked by humorous excesses such as, 'By Jove, Beck, you're fit to be Commander-in-Chief, or Archbishop of Canterbury, by Jove' (p. 196). As Becky writes to Miss Briggs, 'Miss Crawley's Rawdon is *my* Rawdon' (p. 200), and he never again becomes his own Rawdon until after his decisive actions following the confrontation with Steyne.

Rawdon, of course, has already been corrupted by Vanity Fair. Encouraged by Becky, he lives on nothing a year and runs others into debt, delighting in fleecing gulls like George Osborne. But he is 'converted into a very happy and submissive married man' (p. 211), though cut by his aunt as he and Becky drive through the Park. Thackeray gives early hints that Rawdon is not like Becky though; when Becky says that Amelia will cry her eyes out when the regiment has to go abroad, he is 'half angry at his wife's want of feeling' (p. 291). Occasionally he is depressed at the thought of the numerous writs out against him, but Becky has all the wiles to raise his spirits. In Brighton, Rawdon meets Miss Crawley and Briggs out walking, but when he approaches his aunt's door he is afraid to enter, and we observe momentarily a quality of sensitivity hidden beneath his *macho* exterior. Becky, with typical insensitivity, calls him a fool.

When he meets the Osbornes and Jos in Brussels he comes up to them and shakes hands without affectation; and we see a deepening of characterization when Rawdon takes leave of Becky on the eve of the battle. He is moved, and Becky is astute enough to respond with the reactions of simulated grief at his going. He makes an inventory for her, having first told her how much she can get for everything he has:

> My double-barril by Manton, say 40 guineas; my driving cloak, lined with sable fur, £50; my duelling pistols in rosewood case (same which I shot Captain Marker), £20 ... (p. 351)

There are few more sincere expressions of love in *Vanity Fair* than Rawdon's farewell to Becky: 'His face was purple and his eyes dim, as he put her down and left her' (p. 351). Rawdon survives the battle, is promoted to Colonel, and sells out of the army.

In Paris he is an excellent sharper (Peggy O'Dowd's word is 'black-leg' (p. 431)), but Becky decides that he cannot gain an income forever on his accomplished cheating. Before that, their child has been born, and Rawdon's paternal instincts are quickly awakened. He rides over to see his son, who has been put out to nurse near Paris, and his heart 'glowed to see him rosy and dirty, shouting lustily, and happy in the making of mud-pies under the superintendence of the gardener's wife, his nurse' (p. 433). Becky handles his French creditors well; she and Rawdon return to London and continue their swindling and sponging career, though Rawdon feels the slights that Becky endures from fashionable society.

With the advent of Lord Steyne, Rawdon becomes a subsidiary in his own home (or rather, Raggles's), 'not comprehending a word of the jokes, the allusions, the mystical language' (p. 446) or, as Thackeray succinctly puts it, 'He was Colonel Crawley no more. He was Mrs Crawley's husband' (p. 446). He becomes more and more attached to his son, retailing stories of his courage, and there is a particularly moving moment when Rawdon tells the little boy not to cry for fear of waking his mamma. Thackeray's insight here is again true to character: Rawdon, we are told, 'felt somehow ashamed of his paternal softness, and hid it from his wife – only indulging in it when alone with the boy' (p. 449). He blushes red when he and little Rawdon meet old Sedley with little George Osborne, perhaps in memory of his wife's encouragement of Georgy's father, whom he had robbed so regularly.

Later reconciled to his brother through the agency of Becky, Rawdon becomes fond of his sister-in-law, Lady Jane, and asks Becky to get money out of the new Sir Pitt, because 'I should like to give something to old Raggles, hanged if I shouldn't' (p. 518). This marks the onset of conscience, for Rawdon is sickened by their way of life and, doubtless, feels the shadow of Steyne upon them. He feels himself 'more and more isolated every day' (p. 535). Again the author employs his earlier biblical analogy to define Rawdon's state: 'Delilah had imprisoned him, and cut his hair off too' (p. 535). When Becky is presented at Court, Rawdon follows 'in his old Guards' uniform' (p. 555) and ponders on where Becky got her diamonds – he is now increasingly described as 'honest Rawdon'. He takes part in the charades – isn't his own life a charade now? – but is worried by Becky's triumphs:

> They seemed to separate his wife farther than ever from him somehow. He thought with a feeling very like pain how immeasurably she was his superior. (p. 601)

He broods about borrowing Briggs's money, blesses her for her kindness to little Rawdon and feels estranged from Becky, but makes strenuous efforts to keep her from the lures of society. He is impressed by 'Steyne's bounty' (p. 611) towards Briggs, yet is seemingly unaware, man of the world that he is, of the liaison between his wife and that decadent nobleman. Rawdon himself becomes Becky's watch-dog, falling asleep sometimes in her company and waking to find her ever-attentive to his needs. But he is already cuckolded in the mind as well as in the flesh, and the blow which falls – his arrest for debt – finds him writing pathetically to Becky, but being saved by Lady Jane. In his adversity – and how many of Thackeray's characters respond to adversity! – this heavy, stout, forty-five-year-old man responds with a directness of action and spirit. His letter written from Mr Moss's to Becky ends with the words 'God bless you', and the pathetic '*P.S.* – Make haste and come' (p. 616). Faced with the reality of his wife's infidelity and betrayal coupled with the direct insult of Steyne's calling him a 'bully' (p. 620), with its implication that Rawdon has played pimp on Becky's account, he nearly strangles the Lord. He resolves to pay all the debts that he can, and leaves Becky with the justifiable but pathetic words, 'You might have spared me a hundred pounds, Becky, out of all this – I have always shared with you' (p. 621). Mrs Rawdon Crawley's husband has turned; his main concern after this is for his son, but there is a poignant truth in his own self-analysis when he tells his brother:

'I wasn't brought up like a younger brother: but was always encouraged to be extravagant and kept idle. But for this I might have been quite a different man. I didn't do my duty with the regiment so bad.' (p. 625)

He sets aside £600 for Briggs, allocates some money for Becky to get on with, but is forced to forgo his simple idea of moral justice – that of killing Lord Steyne with a ball wrapped in the thousand-pound banknote (p. 626). Forestalled from the duel and pathetically wishing to believe that Becky is innocent, but knowing that she can't be, Rawdon is sad and broken before he goes to Coventry Island. There he later dies, having regularly sent home gifts to Lady Jane, mother in all but name to his son. As I said at the beginning of this section, Rawdon is a triumph, his moral development late but convincing. Again Thackeray employs adversity to show the man outgrowing his vices. He cannot, of course, completely escape the vices of Vanity Fair which have been around him all his life, but Thackeray ensures that he is dispatched far away from scandal at the end.

Jos Sedley

Jos Sedley is a rich caricature. The Collector of Boggley Wollah is vain, shy, pompous, a gourmet, infinitely gullible and a coward – in short, a grotesque, seen almost completely from the outside. Jos entirely lacks a sense of humour, is self-indulgent in dress as well as food and drink, and has little to recommend him to the reader's sympathy. He is an object of mockery to his father, before that gentleman's failure, and Thackeray devotes some time to a retrospective view of his life in India, before presenting him as 'a gay young bachelor' (p. 59) on his return. Jos is the source of much of the humour in the novel, but there is also a sense of pathos, of loneliness and fear, which makes him one of the permanent inhabitants of Vanity Fair. He is lazy, peevish, frightened of women, and this makes Becky's achievement in the early stages all the more remarkable. He is boastful, repetitive and insensitive to others; but pathos never completely deserts him despite, for example, his panic and cowardice in Brussels when he should be taking care of Amelia. Here is the author's early account of his day:

When dressed at length, in the afternoon, he would issue forth to take a drive with nobody in the Park; and then would come back in order to dress again and go and dine with nobody at the Piazza Coffee-House. (pp. 59–60)

Despite the satire, we feel the deprivation. Sensitive about himself to the point of social impotence, he at first feels that Becky may be making fun of him (as indeed she is inwardly), but he enjoys the joke when Becky takes the chili. Jos is a bore, his stories unfunny anecdotes – and he rarely gets to the end of them anyway, so intent is he on eating and drinking. Yet even here we are aware of Thackeray's insight into the psychology of his character: it is perhaps a truism that people eat and drink too much in order to compensate for some lack or failure in themselves, and we should remember that Jos has lived for eight years in India virtually alone, remote from the kind of social life in which he now finds himself.

Becky soon scares him off, but he returns to the fascination; accused by her on his return of being unkind, Jos meditates 'instant departure' (p. 64). But he stays to be flattered by Becky and ridiculed by his father, and the result is that he drunkenly agrees to take the girls to Vauxhall. Becky plays throughout on his vanity (a fitting association with the title of the novel), and he is moved to tell her stories of India, most of them fictitious – for Jos is a born liar, as we see after the Waterloo campaign. He is easily moved and Thackeray even calls him soft-hearted, because he is pro-foundly touched by Becky's singing. Although we cannot see Jos actually proposing, there is a moment when he is very near it before George and Amelia return to the room. Next day he appears with two enormous nosegays for Amelia and Becky, and by his own standards of communi-cation this must be rated as daring. Jos also enjoys being an invalid under the care of Dr Gollop, and one of the funniest moments early in the novel is the picture of him seated close to Becky, his hands bound in her web of green silk, symbolic of the snare she has already cast.

Jos determines to 'pop the question at Vauxhall' (p. 76), and indeed almost tells Amelia of his intentions. 'Almost' is a key word in describing his character, for he brings himself to the brink verbally during the trivia of conversation, as well as in his approaches to Becky. But commitment is beyond him, and rack punch undoes his intentions. The Vauxhall scene, with Jos's singing and uncommon liveliness as 'bold as a lion' (p. 93) he clasps Becky round the waist, is perhaps the funniest in the novel, particu-larly because of the interaction with his mockers who are finally pushed away by Dobbin. The aftermath next morning is pathetic and ludicrous, as Osborne and Dobbin pitilessly expose the events of the previous evening to the prostrate Jos, who readily believes them – 'I believe I'm very terrible, when I'm roused' (p. 96). George in fact succeeds in taking down 'that great hectoring Nabob, and prevent[ing] him from being made a greater fool than he is' (p. 97). Jos, as we would expect, backs away to Cheltenham. It is typical and consistent; but much later, the second time round, Becky makes no mistake.

When his parents' financial crash comes Jos makes them an allowance, but stays in Cheltenham where he is consoled by an Irish widow. He is conveniently clear of the crisis, and since *Vanity Fair* produces a series of crises, we do not see much of him until after Amelia's marriage. He appears at that ceremony to give the bride away, more splendid than ever, and in Brighton he wears 'a military frockcoat' (p. 262) to go with the military appearance and habits he has acquired for the current wave of patriotism. He enjoys moving in the company which includes Becky, plays a few games of billiards with Rawdon, and lives the fiction that he has made for himself – what we might call today the 'military connection'.

His journey to Brussels and the ensuing events are the making of Jos for the future, and the unmaking of his character in the minds of the readers. We are told that 'it served him for conversation for many years after, and even the tiger-hunt story was put aside for more stirring narratives which he had to tell about the great campaign of Waterloo' (p. 323). He suffers on the voyage, but Dobbin gets him a Belgian servant, who calls him 'My Lord', and he soon adapts himself to the situation. Jos is the great boastful patriot who has no idea of what is going on, but whose voice is always heard evaluating the military situation to the advantage of the allies. In Brussels he finds himself accepted by the regiment, indulges himself in his usual fashion, drives about in his carriage and is then left behind as a civilian to look after Amelia.

Thackeray unsparingly describes the extent of Jos's cowardice and self-interest at the advent of war. He is 'in command of the little colony at Brussels' (p. 357), shows his dislike of George now that he is gone and had no idea of what his cunning servant, Isidor, is thinking. The latter brings him continual news of the advance of Napoleon, while Becky plays on his susceptibility by reminding him of how he broke her heart. He is easily duped into believing that she speaks the truth – Becky is of course preparing for the future – but is startled and afraid when he hears the distant gunfire. He panics, tells Mrs O'Dowd to get Amelia ready to go, rages when she won't, and then later hears from Isidor that 'the British army is in full flight' (p. 373). He removes his uniform, has his moustache shaved off by Isidor and pays a small fortune for Becky's horses. Then comes the news of the allied victory, followed by the arrival of Stubble and the further news that the battle is not yet over. Jos orders Amelia to leave, and she refuses, backed by Mrs O'Dowd, who in her turn will not forsake the wounded Stubble. Jos, cowardly and enraged, departs.

He surfaces again in India, where his accounts of Waterloo and his lies about his intimacy with the main figures in the campaign, cause a 'prodigious sensation for some time at Calcutta' (p. 452), and he comes to be known as 'Waterloo Sedley' (p. 452). He makes an allowance of £120 per annum to his parents. When we next see him, some ten years later, he is thinner 'but had gained in majesty and solemnity of demeanour' (p. 666).

He is still vain, and 'took as long a time at his toilette as any fading beauty' (p. 667). His role here is functional, for he is able to assure Dobbin on the voyage to England that Amelia is not married, and thus contribute to that gentleman's rapid recovery of health. On their arrival, Jos shows that he has a temper by refusing to accompany Dobbin in the chaise to London. Instead he makes a leisurely journey there on the third day, stopping at various places and conveying an impression of majesty. Persuaded by Dobbin, he buys a smart chariot for Amelia to drive in and then takes Amelia and his father into his new town house.

He now moves in society, joining the Oriental Club, while his sister entertains on his behalf. He graduates into Court circles too, but his visits to his club are somewhat curtailed by his father's state of health. With old Sedley's death and funeral, Jos reacts as we should expect, retreating to the Star and Garter at Richmond. Later he and Dobbin dine with old Osborne, but it is not until the continental trip that Jos comes fully back into the narrative. At first his mind is absorbed by his proximity to the Earl and Countess of Bareacres, then with leaving his card – and Dobbin's – for 'Our Minister', and then by sleeping and appearing majestically in Pumpernickel. Like his deceased brother-in-law, Jos is a great name-dropper, as he demonstrates in Pumpernickel. He is soon persuaded by Tapeworm's quack that the mineral springs will restore him to 'youth and slimness' (p. 726). He becomes sweet on Gräfinn Fanny de Butterbrod but, remaining behind at the play-table, he meets the masked Becky. He is soon won over by her charm, and considers her virtuous and wronged. Duped again, he tells Amelia that Becky is near to suicide and, more effectively, that little Rawdon was torn from Becky's arms.

Jos is now irretrievably lost, the arrival of the painting convincing him that Becky has always loved him. She goes wherever he goes, gets him to take out life insurance, and Jos confesses to Dobbin that Mrs Crawley would kill him if she knew that he wanted to go back to India, or home with Dobbin. He dies, and Becky gets her share of the money. Again the consistency in the presentation of Jos is evident. There is little or no development in character, because there doesn't need to be. Jos in Russell Square is Jos in Pumpernickel – boastful, snobbish, creating an effect yet unable to sustain it once he opens his mouth, and a moral and physical coward, always invisible in a crisis. Yet his ostentation conceals the timidity and loneliness of his situation and, like so many of Thackeray's characters, the outlines of caricature fade into the indolent, self-indulgent, recognizable traits of character.

Sir Pitt Crawley

One of the finest caricatures in the novel is the disreputable, mean, leering and self-indulgent Baronet, who initiates Becky into 'high life'. I use the latter term comparatively, for this is high life in Hampshire, and it is sordid in the extreme. Sir Pitt's spelling is the first clue to his degraded nature, the second his pestering old Tinker for the 'farden' she has appropriated and the third his frugal supper in which Becky is not invited to partake. Becky's description of him in her first letter to Amelia is worth noting:

> Fancy an old, stumpy, short, vulgar, and very dirty man, in old clothes and shabby old gaiters, who smokes a horrid pipe, and cooks his own horrid supper in a saucepan. (pp. 109–10)

Of course, things are a little more elevated at Queen's Crawley, where Sir Pitt rules his estate by tyranny, has little boys flogged and keeps two bloodhounds on guard at night. He soon begins to take a lecherous interest in Becky, but before that there is a retrospective account of the family in general, and Sir Pitt in particular. His second wife is an iron-monger's daughter, whom he often beats, and he is usually drunk at night. As Thackeray says, 'He had a taste for law' (p. 122), is a sharp landlord and speculates widely and unwisely. His taste for low life consists of drinking and swearing with horse-dealers, farmers and their daughters; Thackeray asserts that there was no one 'more cunning, mean, selfish, foolish, disreputable' than Sir Pitt (p. 123). His irony plays over the exalted position held by this nearly illiterate boor in the ranks of Vanity Fair.

Sir Pitt manifests jealousy when he sees Becky and Rawdon talking together, but is too insensitive and ignorant to think much about it. With the death of his wife he immediately hurries to propose to Becky. It is far from romantic, though it is of course lecherous and self-interested, since Sir Pitt knows Becky's worth to him – 'You've got more brains in your little vinger than any baronet's wife in the county' (p. 186). When Becky tells him that she is already married, he assumes that her husband has left her, and unscrupulously invites her to be his mistress. Sir Pitt enjoys the joke hideously, but in fact the joke is on him; when he learns that Becky has married his son he is 'wild with hatred and insane with baffled desire' (p. 203). Later he bursts into Becky's room and flings about her clothes and papers.

We meet him some time afterwards, when he 'had given himself up entirely to his bad courses, to the great scandal of the county and the mute horror of his son' (p. 390). Everyone expects him to marry Miss Horrocks, the butler's daughter, but he becomes steadily more befuddled and 'unshorn' (p. 469). He takes a liking to Lady Jane, mocks his son Pitt and makes Lady Jane a present of some pearls, receiving a lecture from Miss Horrocks afterwards for this indiscretion. She now rules him, and 'the Baronet's daily perplexities increased, and his embarrassments multiplied round him' (p. 471). He is still able to laugh at her 'assumptions of dignity and imitations of genteel life' (p. 472). He drinks a great quantity of rum-and-water with Horrocks and goes into a stupor the same night.

The 'Christian carnivora' (George Eliot's phrase) arrive in the form of Mrs Bute, her husband and son. Sir Pitt's last days have some alleviation, for Lady Jane walks with him and he moans when she has to leave. The author's words, as he tells us how the old man cries when he is pushed away from the fire, sum up his base life:

> For this was all that was left after more than seventy years of cunning and struggling, and drinking and scheming, and sin and selfishness – a whimpering old idiot put in and out of bed and cleaned and fed like a baby. (p. 478)

Pitt (later Sir Pitt) Crawley

Anyone less like his father than Pitt Crawley it would be hard to imagine. His father was a boor – Pitt is a bore. He was at one time Private Secretary to Lord Binkie, then an attaché in Pumpernickel, but retires to become a country gentleman. He is active in matters as various as the question of Negro Emancipation and Malt, writing a pamphlet on the latter, and he subjects the servants to devotional exercises. He virtually runs the Hall, having advanced his father money, and patronizes an Independent 'meeting-house in the Crawley parish' (p. 121). He is rigid and austere in manner, treating Becky with politeness and, later, a great deal of respect, for he is not immune either to her charm or her formidable persuasive ability. He treats the second Lady Crawley, who is only an ironmonger's daughter, with deference, and Sir Pitt is somewhat in awe of him because of the loan he has accepted.

He is politically ambitious, and tries to persuade his father to yield his seat in Parliament to him. What is quite remarkable is that Lady Jane Sheepshanks should be attracted to someone who was known as 'Miss Crawley' at Eton. He cannot really cope with Becky, who consults him on passages of French, deludes him about the nature of the children's education and doubtless laughs in her sleeve at his piety ('What is money compared to our souls, sir?' (p. 130)). In a sense he gets his reward, for Becky and Mrs Bute between them manage to alienate Miss Crawley.

Before Miss Crawley's death, Pitt contrives to ingratiate himself with Lady Southdown, and persuades that impressive and dedicated lady to visit Miss Crawley – the result being that Lady Jane is soon established in Miss Crawley's favour.

The latter leaves the bulk of her money to Pitt, who has a difficult time while Miss Horrocks rules his father. But he succeeds to the title and is able to indulge a new sense of power, even putting Lady Southdown in her place. Later he stays with Rawdon and Becky in Curzon Street, is enchanted with Becky's cooking, which is much better than Lady Jane's, and responds to her flattery and coddling by inviting his brother and Becky to Hampshire for Christmas. At the back of his mind he knows that he ought to give Rawdon something – that he is his brother's debtor. He vacillates about this, becoming increasingly aware of his own position and wishing to make his way in politics and society, even becoming more orthodox in his Christianity. He also allows himself to believe Becky, who says that she intends to help him towards the position in the world which his talents deserve. He changes his way of life and, more particularly, his social manners:

> Therefore it was that this roguish diplomatist had grown so hospitable; that he was so civil to oratorios and hospitals; so kind to Deans and Chapters; so generous in giving and accepting dinners; so uncommonly gracious to farmers on market-days; and so much interested about county business ... (p. 529)

He has yielded himself up to Vanity Fair. He gives Rawdon £100, assiduously attends Parliament, studies Blue Books and dresses in his diplomatic uniform – thus giving Becky a subject for impersonation, which she uses to divert Lord Steyne. Sir Pitt goes to Court (he has rashly given Becky a diamond clasp) and also attends the celebrated charades, though he disapproves of Becky's behaviour. When Rawdon goes to him on the night after the confrontation with Steyne (remember that it was Sir Pitt's money, brought by Lady Jane, which purchased Rawdon's freedom from his creditors), he proves to have more generosity of spirit than we should have thought and agrees to watch over little Rawdon. Ultimately the latter is made his heir.

When Becky throws herself at his feet in mitigation of her behaviour, Sir Pitt is amazed at his wife's outburst (he is still under Becky's spell) and promises to try and effect a reconciliation between her and Rawdon. Lady Jane triumphs, however, and Pitt's mind is 'poisoned against' Becky (p. 739) by Mr Wenham. Despite a high degree of sincerity, there is something of the fool in Sir Pitt and therefore no reason to believe that he is destined for success. In fact he loses both his Parliamentary seats after the Reform Bill (1832), and being 'both out of pocket and out of spirits by that catastrophe, failed in his health, and prophesied the speedy ruin of the Empire' (pp. 793–4).

Lady Crawley (née Sheepshanks)

Lady Jane is one of the most likeable characters in *Vanity Fair*. She is a true Christian in principle and practice, having been strictly brought up by 'Lady Macbeth' (in reality Lady Southdown) on tracts and 'bodily medicament' (p. 392), and pines for her brother who, after serious beginnings, had succumbed to the lures of Vanity Fair in the form of visits to the opera, smoking cigars, and drinking curaçao. Lady Jane is twenty-six when we first meet her, and is devoted to her mother and sister, the latter a poet who is obsessed by the sufferings of the native populations. Her father loved Lady Jane, but he was an epileptic and died. Lady Jane makes an immediate impression upon Miss Crawley, and 'accompanied her in her drives, and solaced many of her evenings' (p. 399). She is so genuinely good that she does not inspire jealousy (except in Becky), and even agrees to play piquet with Miss Crawley, although it is against her principles. There is no hypocrisy in this, just a warm desire to please the wicked old lady who is soon to die. When she marries Pitt they live with Miss Crawley, who settles her money on them, endures the tyranny of Lady Southdown and becomes completely dependent on Lady Jane. The latter is so generous in spirit that she expects her husband to share the old lady's legacy with Rawdon. Old Sir Pitt responds to her immediately, and gives her the pearls which had originally belonged to his mother.

She writes to invite Becky to the Hall, greets her warmly, 'kissed her affectionately' (p. 487), and at first is completely duped by Becky, telling her husband 'that she thought her new sister-in-law was a kind, frank, unaffected, and affectionate young woman' (p. 490). Lady Jane is devoted to her children, and begins to see through Becky, one suspects, when young Rawdon reveals to her that at home he dines in the kitchen, and later says to his mother, 'You never kiss me at home, mamma' (p. 530). Her sweetness, kindness and goodness soon come under Becky's baleful scrutiny. Lady Jane is also timid, but rather resents the fact that her husband discusses things with Becky that he doesn't discuss with her. She finds that she can't continue to read stories to the children in Becky's presence. She knows, too, 'that Rebecca had captivated her husband' (p. 536), but when they go to Court for Sir Pitt's presentation Lady Jane good-naturedly insists that it should be a family party.

She is able to laugh at Becky's assumption of grandeur, but deplores her own inadequate taste, feeling completely eclipsed by that unscrupulous little minx. Lady Jane is, however, capable of independent action, as she demonstrates when she takes the £100 to free Rawdon, Sir Pitt being away at a Parliamentary dinner. She 'puts her kind hand in his' (p. 619) and gives Rawdon new hope. The following day she finds Becky at Sir Pitt's feet; in a spirited and unequivocal passion she damns Becky as 'a heartless mother, a false wife' (p. 638) and threatens to leave the house with her children if that woman – 'She is not worthy to sit down with Christian people' (p. 638) – remains.

With the death of the sickly Pitt Binkie from whooping-cough and measles, Rawdon becomes heir to Queen's Crawley, and movingly acknowledges, 'Oh, Aunt Jane, you are my mother!' (p. 740). The final words about her reveal her close friendship with Amelia and Dobbin, who name their daughter after her; the Baronet – the little Rawdon we have known – lives with her at Queen's Crawley. Lady Jane does not cloy and there is sufficient development, particularly in her spirit, to move her from idealized caricature to character. In a very deliberate sense, Thackeray has made her the unsung heroine of *Vanity Fair*.

Miss Crawley

Everyone pays court to Miss Crawley, the half-sister of old Sir Pitt, because of her money. She likes Rawdon because of his rakish qualities, and has paid his debts at college, as well as indicating that he will have a half-share in her will. She is a domestic tyrant, expressing her likes and dislikes forcibly; she considers Pitt a 'milksop' (p. 129) and when she visits Queen's Crawley his sermons have to be abandoned. She is a Radical, interested in women's rights, the subject of divorce and all things French, but a hypocrite, conservative in her judgement and standards, as Becky and Rawdon find out to their cost. One of her Radical eccentricities is that she has pictures of Mr Fox in every room in the house.

She is silly and romantic as well as being apoplectic, but she has a fine sense of humour, referring to Briggs as her 'toady' (p. 136) and in fact delighted at being toadied to anyway. She is a natural blackmailer, threatening to leave 'her money to the Shropshire Crawleys' (p. 137) if anyone at the Hall offends her. Beneath all this there lies (as we saw with Jos Sedley) the pathos of loneliness and suspicion. Becky naturally wins the 'heart of that good-natured London rake' (p. 141) who, irony of ironies, wishes that someone would run away with Becky, little suspecting that that is precisely what will happen.

Miss Crawley is a semi-invalid, largely because of her own capacity to drink and eat to excess. She allows Becky to displace Briggs in her Park

Lane house, and thoroughly enjoys Becky's impersonations of that long-suffering female. She displays some temper after Becky has refused Sir Pitt, asking her 'are you waiting for the Prince Regent's divorce, that you don't think our family good enough for you?' (p. 189). Again, the irony of this remark is apparent, because she is in fact 'mollified by the girl's refusal' (p. 190) – an ominous comment on Becky's and Rawdon's hopes. Becky's hints at an affair find the old lady greatly moved, and she embraces Becky 'with an almost maternal kindness' (p. 192).

The arrival of Mrs Bute and the coincidence of Becky's elopement throw the old lady first into hysterics and then into Mrs Bute's willing arms. Her recovery is hindered by the constant ministrations of Mrs Bute, whose severity undermines Miss Crawley, who now has to endure 'Mrs Bute reading books of devotion to her' (p. 228). She also has to listen to Mrs Bute's detailed researches on Rawdon's and Becky's behaviour, and these of course condition her responses to the couple. But she begins to hate Mrs Bute, even though when driving in the Park she cuts Rawdon dead. The accident of Bute breaking his collarbone changes everything; when Mrs Bute leaves, Miss Crawley soon reverts to her old habits.

She is astute enough to see through Rawdon's letters and register the hand that really wrote them. Although she allows Rawdon to visit her – she will never see Becky again – she accuses Briggs of allowing herself to be bribed by him. She also refuses to see Mrs Bute, and gives Rawdon a mere twenty pounds. After Waterloo, Becky once more seeks a return to favour by sending Miss Crawley souvenirs of the battle, which she bought from one of the many pedlars who deal in such wares, and purporting to come from Rawdon's own experiences in the campaign. Rawdon's promotion fails to move her, and she becomes very bitter when Becky gains an entrée into Parisian society through the use of her name.

James Crawley's smoking habits offend her too, since the smell won't let her sleep, but the announcement of the birth of a son to Rawdon and Becky exasperates her beyond measure. She autocratically orders Pitt to marry Lady Jane, thus making his fortune for him. They stay with her and she clings to Lady Jane, just as her brother is later to rely on that kind-hearted and genuine woman. Lady Southdown rules her towards the end of her life, and she grows increasingly timid. Despite her tyranny in life, she leaves Briggs an annuity, which is later swindled out of her by Becky. Thackeray refers to 'the last scene of her dismal Vanity Fair comedy' (p. 306), and her 'scream of hysterical tears' (p. 306) emphasizes the pathos of her situation. We might remember that although her sufferings are largely of her own making, it is her money which ensures her unhappiness.

Mrs Bute Crawley

Mrs Bute is a practical, gossipy, manipulating kind of woman, small, dark-eyed and intense. She has six children, and seeks to provide for them by undermining the position of other members of the family – particularly that of Rawdon – with Miss Crawley. With the arrival of Becky at the Hall Mrs Bute is constantly on the alert, and writes to Miss Pinkerton about her, including the cunning reference to Becky in an apparently casual postscript.

Becky waxes satirical about her in the second letter to Amelia, describing her as 'a little, black-faced old woman in a turban, rather crooked, and with very twinkling eyes' (p. 138). Becky of course sees through Mrs Bute's interrogations of her, but that lady is intent on having her son, James, in Miss Crawley's will, and works towards that end. She thinks that her husband is a fool, and demonstrates her own capacity for deviousness when she tells Rawdon that Becky will soon be his mother-in-law. Mrs Bute is gambling that if anything does happen between Becky and Rawdon, Miss Crawley won't come round. She is right, and indeed arrives at the opportune moment, after Briggs has received Becky's letter announcing her marriage to Rawdon. But, to continue the gambling metaphor, Mrs Bute overplays her hand: her regimen is too strict for Miss Crawley. What Mrs Bute does succeed in doing is completely discrediting Becky and Rawdon with the old lady. Her researches, as ever, are assiduous, and she uncovers enough information to ensure that the supposedly Radical old lady will never receive Becky again. The retailing of gossip, mixed with her sermons, show what a hypocritical woman she is. She works to turn Miss Crawley's ill-health to her advantage, and only fate stops her. As we have seen, Miss Crawley has begun to hate Mrs Bute's tyranny, and the medical attendants fear her influence on Miss Crawley (Squills calls her 'a little harpy' (p. 234)).

Her husband's broken collarbone catches her, so to speak, in full stride. She hastens home and later dispatches James, who is too much his father's son to succeed with Miss Crawley. Mrs Bute quickly realizes that Pitt and Lady Jane are making inroads into Miss Crawley's sympathies but, rightly, has little faith in James's success with his unpredictable aunt. After her death Bute only gets £5,000, but Mrs Bute, ever resilient, adapts well to the circumstances and tries to marry off her daughters by 'drilling them rigidly hour after hour' (p. 468) in duets and the fine art of attracting suitors. Such is Vanity Fair, that they act as if they have inherited their aunt's money.

Her ever-present intelligence from the Hall enables her to step over there sharply in her 'black calash' (p. 474), have Miss Horrocks incarcerated in the strong room, virtually dismiss Horrocks and show herself mistress of the situation. When Pitt succeeds to the title, Mrs Bute meets Becky again and is forced to tolerate her, but she effectively fades from the action. Her spirit is shown when she reads in the newspapers of Becky's presentation at Court. She tells her eldest daughter with something approaching satire:

> 'If you had been sandy-haired, green-eyed, and a French rope-dancer's daughter
> ... you might have had superb diamonds forsooth, and have been presented at
> Court by your cousin, Lady Jane. But you're only a gentlewoman, my poor dear
> child. You have only some of the best blood in England in your veins, and good
> principles and piety for your portion.' (p. 561)

We note this as a true and searching comment on Vanity Fair, but Mrs Bute's self-righteousness and over-articulate virtue make her, ironically, part of it.

Bute Crawley

Mrs Crawley's husband is something of a caricature. He rowed in the Christchurch boat at Oxford, loves all sports, gambles, rides to hounds, sings well, fishes better and is always in debt. As the younger brother he automatically becomes the Rector, though in terms of faith and personality he is singularly unsuited to the task, and his wife writes his sermons. He fears that his brother, Sir Pitt, will sell the reversion to his living, which means that his son James – also totally unsuitable to be a Rector – will not succeed him. He loathes Rawdon, but is brought round by his wife, since he lacks depth and is really only interested in sport and betting. He inconveniently breaks his collarbone, thus effectively depriving his family of any chance of Miss Crawley's money; and we learn later that James does succeed him in the living.

Young Rawdon Crawley and Young George Osborne

The two boys reflect the parallelism in characterization which Thackeray employs, contrasting Amelia and Becky, Rawdon and George (and Dobbin); but in the presentation of the children he shows an admirable sense of family consistency and acute psychological insight. Little George, for example, is thoroughly cared for and even molly-coddled by his mother and subsequently enjoys the patronage of his grandfather. In spite of this, he perhaps comes to value Dobbin more than anybody, as we see when he cries after Dobbin has left. Rawdon, in contrast, is neglected by his mother, idolized by his father and has to show particular courage at school and at home in order not to offend his mother. He speaks out when he goes to Queen's Crawley, putting his mother in her place by his honesty about her lack of affection for him.

Thackeray is showing the influence, as I have said earlier, of both nature and nurture. The spoiled little George, with his selfishness and lack of concern for his mother, reflects the identical qualities found in his father: there is also every evidence he too is a social climber. Rawdon, by contrast, is brought up by Briggs and the surreptitious attentions of his father, ultimately finding an adoptive mother in Lady Jane. He seems, too, to be influenced by the developing decency of his father, just as George is influenced favourably by his adoptive father, Dobbin. George, who lords it over his grandfather, is not without some generosity of heart; he buys his mother a miniature of himself (but it *is* of *himself*) and, as far as we can gather, develops well under the tutelage of Dobbin, who impresses the young man with his own standards and integrity. Dobbin had, in fact, had the same effect on his father.

Rawdon has a worse childhood than George, since he at first worships Becky, who visits him infrequently, but who becomes merely a beautiful vision to him. He loves to hear her sing, and has his ears boxed for doing so when she is entertaining Lord Steyne. The latter can't stand the boy, who always eats in the kitchen and receives what kindness he gets from his father's clandestine visits to the nursery, with Briggs and the servants making much of this attractive child. When he goes to Queen's Crawley he gets his first taste of hunting and attaches himself to Lady Jane. This attachment is lifelong, for he not only inherits Queen's Crawley, but stays there with Lady Jane and her daughter. Thackeray is particularly good at presenting children; one recalls his own drawings of his children, the love and attention he gave them, his pride in them and, perhaps most poign antly, their lack of a mother. He realizes only too well the nature of heredity, the dangers of possessiveness and the results of neglect. Both children are presented convincingly and, best of all, without sentiment.

Mr Sedley

In Amelia's father Thackeray traces the decline from prosperity to poverty with its inevitable effects on character. When we first meet him in Russell Square, Sedley is an attractive character, so much so that it is hard to see any resemblance between him and Jos, for example, or even Amelia. On his first appearance he walks in 'rattling his seals like a true

British merchant' (p. 56). He teases Jos, at times mercilessly, and immediately sees through Becky's intentions towards Jos, telling his wife to give her some curry and bursting into coarse laughter when she takes the chili. As the author points out, they love practical jokes on the Stock Exchange, and perhaps the irony is that life gets beyond a joke for Mr Sedley, who warns Jos about Becky. He is good-natured, bears no ill-will to Becky, and even tells his wife that he would welcome her – 'The girl's a white face at any rate. *I* don't care who marries him' (p. 68) – and is generous to her when she leaves.

But as the international situation worsens, so his own position declines. Sedley is made a bankrupt, and all the possessions in Russell Square are sold. His moving confession of his failure to his wife, telling her that they must begin all over again, is undercut by the fact that he has previously kept her in ignorance of his affairs. In six weeks he ages more than he had in fifteen years and what rankles him most of all, of course, is the behaviour of John Osborne, whom he had set up in business. For a while he is entirely 'prostrate in the ruins of his own affairs and shattered honour' (p. 218). After the move to Fulham he tries his hand at a number of ventures, all of which fail; he goes out and about to convince himself and his wife that he is still in business. He is as opposed to Amelia's match with George as old Osborne and refuses to attend the wedding. There is a rare pathos as he tries so desperately to keep up appearances, and Dobbin is much moved 'by the sight of this once kind old friend, crazed almost with misfortune and raving with senile anger' (p. 242). For Sedley, who 'used to go of nights to a little club at a tavern, where he disposed of the finances of the nation' (p. 453), the taste of poverty is bitter.

He takes little Georgy for walks, on one occasion meeting Rawdon and his son. He is dependent on the kindness of Clapp, in whose house he lives and who was once his clerk. He has recourse to a moneylender in the City, and Jos's annuity to the family is paid away. Again there is a moving moment when he confesses this to Amelia, and she responds kindly to her father, though she knows that with their circumstances so depleted, Georgy must now go to old Osborne.

After her mother's death, Amelia tries to make her father happy. He becomes very fond of her and completely dependent on her; when Dobbin returns we find that the old man is 'prattling away according to his wont, with some old story about old times' (p. 677). Sedley is badly shaken, much affected by the return of Jos, and is restored to some kind of social position in his own mind when he drives about in the carriage with Amelia. He soon becomes very ill and clings to Amelia, conscious of his past bitterness towards her for marrying George. His last words are, 'O Emmy, I've been thinking we were very unkind and unjust to you' (p. 702).

Thackeray makes this good man's decline and fall a comment on the nature of Vanity Fair, and it is a radical comment at that; he had 'no chance of revenge against Fortune, which had had the better of him' (p. 703).

Mrs Sedley

Mrs Sedley plays little part in the main action of the novel before the move to Fulham. She is fond of Jos but wishes he were not so shy, and leads a life of ease and comfort before the financial collapse. When told by her husband that Becky is setting out to captivate Jos, she is at first critical of Becky and then won over to her by her husband's influence. She takes him to task for his mockery of Jos, feels a little 'maternal jealousy' (p. 68) of Becky, but is so good-natured and easy-going that this soon passes, and she is embarrassed when Becky leaves. Her self-absorption is such that she has no conception of her husband's suffering until his confession. That confession elicits a response at which Sedley himself is amazed. She takes 'the office of consoler':

> She took his trembling hand, and kissed it, and put it round her neck; she called him John – her dear John – her old man – her kind old man; she poured out a hundred words of incoherent love and tenderness ... (p. 215)

This illustrates Thackeray's strong identification with Mrs Sedley, and the reality of her life with her husband; she believes that the news 'will break Emmy's heart' (p. 215).

She speaks bitterly to Dobbin of the old times when the Osbornes had been glad to have their help, but conspires with him to bring George and Amelia together. She indulges the romance and sentiment of it, sobs in her pew during the ceremony, and takes 'an hysterical adieu of her daughter' (p. 260). When Amelia comes home again after her honeymoon, Mrs Sedley laughs and cries with her and prepares her a muffin and marmalade. Later her life in Fulham is described – 'She was content to lie on the shore where Fortune had stranded her' (p. 454), gossiping with her landlady and making a life of tradesmen and neighbours sufficient to her small needs. She is unwise enough to administer Daffy's Elixir to little George, and this prompts a raging quarrel between her and Amelia. She insists that Amelia has called her a murderess, adopts the attitude of a tragedy queen and doesn't speak to Amelia for weeks afterwards.

It would be true to say that she enjoys the distance she has created, but it is a sad compensation – a meanness fashioned by the poverty in which she lives. She also wishes that Amelia would consider Dobbin, and is angry beyond measure when her daughter buys books for Georgy 'when the whole house wants bread!' (p. 543). She tells Amelia that she is ruining her son while her father is without a shilling. Mrs Sedley becomes increasingly embittered as their debts get worse, forgoes her conversations with her landlady, Mrs Clapp, because she owes her so much money, and carps at Amelia for 'her silly pride in her child, and her neglect of her parents' (p. 574). Though their position improves once Georgy goes to his grandfather, it is only a few months before the old lady takes to her bed and dies, tenderly watched over by Amelia but resentful of her daughter to the end. Once again the deprivations of poverty are reflected in the change from a kind-hearted, good-natured woman to an embittered and lonely one.

John Osborne

The father of George is a tyrant. He is always scowling, has great pride in the family – hence the Osborne coat of arms – and rules his daughters while spoiling and indulging his son, though being unceasingly critical of him. As Sedley's affairs worsen – and the worst of his creditors is Osborne himself, whom he had set up in life many years ago – Osborne becomes insistent that George break off his long-standing engagement to Amelia. He greets Amelia rudely, and 'dropped the little hand out of his great hirsute paw without any attempt to hold it there' (p. 161), an anticipation of his later letter to her. His glance follows her out of the room as if she is guilty of something, though he mellows a little to his son's deliberate name-dropping, for old Osborne is one of the worst kind of snobs. As the author puts it, 'Whenever he met a great man he grovelled before him, and my-lorded him as only a free-born Briton can do' (p. 164). He tells his son that unless he sees Amelia's dowry (£10,000), George shall not marry her.

He worships money, but has no real happiness in it. He is ungenerously acquisitive, particularly of power, and ruins his elder daughter's chances of happiness with the artist, Smee, being determined that she shall act as housekeeper to him. Before that he writes a brutal letter to Amelia, telling her that 'her father's conduct had been of such a nature that all engagements between the families were at an end' (p. 218). This shows the tyrannical nature of the man, and the cowardly aspect of this action means that we can have no sympathy for old Osborne. In Vanity Fair the strong survive, while the weak go to the wall.

Thackeray is explicit about the nature of Osborne's rule – 'He called kicking a footman downstairs, a hint to the latter to leave his service' (p.

249). His determination that George will marry Miss Swartz is reinforced by blackmail, and since he has no delicacy of feeling he doesn't hesitate to carry out his threats. He stands slightly in awe of George because the latter has the manners of a gentleman, something which he has failed to acquire. His quarrel with George shows his irascibility and unscrupulousness, combining to ensure that he will be embittered for the rest of his days – there is a kind of poetic justice about this fact. When Dobbin comes to see him he speaks of himself as working like a convict, saying that he will make George a Colonel, for he obviously believes that money can buy anything. Shut in his room afterwards, he gives himself up to all the bitterness of thwarted ambition, going through his son's papers and then obliterating his name from the family Bible. In this obdurate mood he burns his will, and next day makes a new one. The expression on his face is 'ghastly and worn' (p. 282), but during the day he is particularly gentle and quiet.

His letter to George from his lawyer stresses that there is to be no further communication between them. This finality is to increase his bitterness later. He is 'borne down by his fate and sorrow' (p. 416) with the news of George's death, perhaps worsened by the fact that he will tell no one of his sufferings. When Alderman Dobbin delivers George's final letter to old Osborne he is further stricken, but his spirit is aroused by George's asking him to care for his wife and, perhaps, her child. He has a memorial erected to George, goes to Brussels, drives about the battlefield, is told that Dobbin brought his son's body back to Brussels, sees Amelia in the carriage and knows that 'He hated her' (p. 422). When Dobbin pleads with him on Amelia's account he refuses, saying he has 'sworn never to speak to that woman, or to recognize her as his son's wife' (p. 424).

His subsequent ageing is pathetic as well as violent; and when his daughter Maria marries Frederick Bullock, he is only invited to their third-rate parties, thus being made keenly aware of his social inferiority. He boasts about his money, drives out Smee, brings Jane to subjection and then learns from her that she has seen little George and that he is just like his father. When he sees Georgy old Osborne trembles, formally offers to take the boy and then is insulting enough to add that Amelia's allowance will not be withdrawn should she marry again. Amelia's surrender to his wishes finds Osborne in a generous mood, but it is a generosity tainted with a sadistic streak: he enjoys the humiliation the Sedleys must now suffer in order to survive on his money. He spoils George unremittingly, and is patronized by the boy just as he had been patronized by the father before him. The boy assesses him as a 'dullard' (p. 649), but his grandfather takes great pride in his fights, in his getting tipsy and in his stories. Thackeray puts it succinctly when he says 'In Russell Square everybody was afraid of Mr Osborne, and Mr Osborne was afraid of Georgy' (p. 658).

Towards the end of his life, Osborne relents. He has Dobbin and Jos ostentatiously to dinner, questions Dobbin about Amelia, comes to respect Dobbin more and more for his honesty and loyalty, and a reconciliation with Amelia is planned. It never takes place, for old Osborne dies, striving to speak at the end. His will shows 'that the hatred which he had so long cherished had gone out of his heart' (p. 708). Amelia receives an annuity of £500 and resumes the guardianship of the boy.

Old Osborne's death enables the author to bring Amelia into comfortable social circumstances, but one wonders at Osborne's change of mind, or rather of heart, for there has been no preparation for this. He is a scoundrel, a moral blackguard, unscrupulous, sadistic, thoroughly selfish, ignorant and unsympathetic, with false standards and ideas of grandeur. All this viciousness changes, but it is difficult for the reader to accept the change. Perhaps it is that near death he repents, but there is no reason to suppose that old Osborne believes himself to be dying. The contrast between himself and Sedley is marked, but he is given a family consistency with his son and grandson. He is something of a grotesque, offering for Miss Swartz himself not, like George, being particular about colour, but only caring about 'tin'.

Other Characters

The richness of *Vanity Fair* is largely due to the range of characters covered by Thackeray in his comprehensive presentation of society. **James Crawley** appears only briefly in a telling chapter which describes his misguided approaches to his aunt. He has run up a number of bills at Oxford, brings gifts of produce from Mrs Bute (as well as his favourite bull-dog, Towzer) and has grown up into a handsome young man. Miss Crawley pays his bill at the hotel and to Pitt's chagrin invites him to stay with her. James is interested in all sports, like his father (and Rawdon before him), and is discomforted when he and his aunt see the two boxers, the Tutbury Pet and the Rottingdean Fibber, whom he had patronized the previous evening. He is obviously embarrassed by the standard of behaviour expected of him in his aunt's society. His tongue is quickly loosened, however, when he is plied with drink, and he reveals his belief in blood ('I'm none of your radicals' (p. 407)), drawing an unsuitable analogy, perhaps the only one he knows, with dogs killing rats. When the gentlemen rejoin the ladies he is palpably put out, but worse is to come; he has drunk so much gin the previous evening in the company of his boxing friends, that the bill which Miss Crawley has offered to pay offends her. Jim cannot retrieve his ground; his bulldog attacks Miss Crawley's Blenheim spaniel, he goes tipsily to bed and then smokes, the tobacco fumes giving Miss Crawley a sleepless night. It is the final blow and, although Jim is caricature, we note once again Thackeray's consistency – he is sufficiently like his father to be credible.

Peggy O'Dowd, the **Major**, later **Colonel**, and **Glorvina O'Dowd** (later **Posky**) are brilliantly created, with Peggy taking pride of place. Her real name is Auralia Margaretta; she is vivacious, warm, loquacious and the subject of much mockery (and she knows it) by George Osborne. But she is good-natured, her one real object in life being to get her sister Glorvina married. Her greatest attributes are her kindness, her loyalty and her courage. She looks after Amelia both physically and emotionally, though George, of course, doesn't think she is good enough to mix with his wife. Her friendliness is manifested at once, when she invites Amelia to a small evening party, and her jolliness, vivacity and rich Irish brogue are all endearing. Even more endearing is her no-nonsense attitude; she has no use for a social climber like Becky, and her preparations for her husband's departure to the battlefield are a moving testimony to her warmth, love and practicality. She is a religious woman, talks pedigrees much of the time, and knows everything about everybody else in the regiment. A dominating character, Peggy O'Dowd drinks beer, wears a very large 'repayther' on her stomach, is intensely proud of her native Ireland and talks irrelevances on the eve of momentous events. She is boastful without being offensive, and she provides great amusement even for someone as sober as Dobbin. She begins to be impatient of George's neglect of Amelia, but soon has to exert herself on her husband's account.

Mrs O'Dowd always reads her uncle the Dean's sermons on important occasions, is rather upset when left alone, but hastens to comfort Amelia at the instigation, ironically, of Becky. She is contemptuous of Jos's flight, saying that she won't desert Amelia or leave 'till O'Dowd gives me the route' (p. 371). She watches by the wounded Ensign Stubble, and by the sick Amelia, reads from her sermons and prays for her husband. She treats Stubble like a child – there is something movingly maternal in her care of him – and Jos like a coward, which he is. She even finds time to laugh at herself and, later moved to Madras, is the same as she always was and will be. As the author puts it – and it is an admirable summary of what we have seen so far –

Peggy O'Dowd is indeed the same as ever; kind in act and thought: impetuous in temper: eager to command: a tyrant over her Michael: a dragon amongst all the ladies of the regiment: a mother to all the young men, whom she tends in their sickness, defends in all their scrapes ... (p. 507)

Lady Peggy is very popular, as we should expect, alternately 'the best of comforters' and 'the most troublesome of friends' (p. 507). She is determined that Dobbin will marry Glorvina, but Dobbin withstands the assault, Peggy only exacerbating the position by her criticism of Mrs Osborne. She is full of life and undoubtedly one of the most vivid caricatures in *Vanity Fair*.

Her husband, we are told, agrees with everybody. He is a sheep-faced and meek little man, inevitably good-humoured and unruffled wherever he goes. He is also unquestionably brave, performing many acts of gallantry during the course of his rising career. His prediction about the battle of Waterloo, uttered to Peggy while he 'placidly pulled his nightcap over his ears' (p. 347), is that 'there will be such a ball danced in a day or two as some of 'em has never heard the chune of' (p. 347). When he is made ready by his own and Peggy's ministrations, he inspires confidence and cheerfulness in those he is commanding. Sir Michael, as he becomes, doesn't allow himself to be browbeaten over the question of a match between Glorvina and Dobbin, saying that the latter is big enough to choose for himself and even warning Dobbin that 'them girls is bent on mischief' (p. 510). Dobbin, however, escapes to England.

Glorvina is pure caricature, appearing in finery and curlpapers, dancing with subalterns and riding. But her satin cannot win Dobbin, and she later becomes the wife of Major Posky, 'having resolved never to marry out of the regiment' (p. 793).

Of the other minor characters two stand out – **Briggs** and **Lady Southdown**. The former is Miss Crawley's companion, who is first displaced by Becky and then won over to her side. We find her confiding in Firkin when Becky assumes power and she has lost her beloved friend Matilda. She is so insecure that she tolerates Becky's mimicry of her to her face; but a lifetime of devotion to Miss Crawley is repaid by a legacy. That legacy, of course, is swallowed by Becky and Rawdon, but Rawdon later repays Briggs for her care of his son. She is a querulous woman, at her best when serving others, and she is gullible to the point of being ridiculous. Becky decides to send the letter announcing her elopement with Rawdon to Briggs, for she knows that this good-hearted, sentimental female will be overcome by the romance of the situation. Indeed Briggs tries to get Becky and Rawdon back into favour after Waterloo, but to no avail. She is later the 'watch-dog' employed by Becky as cover for her affair with Steyne, who hates her. She also takes care of little Rawdon, whose mother despises him.

Lady Southdown is larger than life, a woman who rules until Pitt stands up to her after his inheritance. She has dominated her daughters and her son becomes relatively dissolute. Her daughter, Lady Emily, writes poems and hymns, and Lady Jane obeys her mother in all things until her marriage. Her spheres of interest are medical and religious, and she considers herself an authority in each. A genuine eccentric, she distributes tracts, takes over the dying Miss Crawley and provides Becky with one of her most memorable impersonations. She strongly disapproves of her son-in-law's orthodoxy, and writes to Lady Emily about Lady Jane's worldliness.

The remaining characters can be dealt with briefly. **Maria Osborne** marries **Frederick Bullock** after some difficulty, because of her father's obstinacy over settlements and a disagreement with Bullock's firm. She becomes a social climber in the true Osborne tradition, outdistancing and indeed deliberately effacing old Osborne, whose crude and coarse behaviour does not fit him to move in her refined circle. She makes up to Amelia after the latter has been left money, and because of young George's substantial inheritance. She is distinctly like her father and George – egoistic and determined.

Her sister **Jane** at first thinks that Dobbin is making up to her and, when she feels she has been used, is singularly cool to that gentleman when she sees him some years later before her father's death. She appears more tremulous and impressionable than her sister and father, perhaps more like George in terms of immediate susceptibility. She bursts into tears when she tells her father that she has seen little George, is frustrated in her romance with the artist, and lives a lonely life as housekeeper in her father's gloomy house, where she will not be persuaded to stay after his death.

The upstairs-downstairs quality that I have referred to throughout this study is observable in such vivid vignettes as **Firkin**, who consoles Briggs, and **Isidor**, who dupes the cowardly Jos in Brussels and has one of the funniest scenes in the novel. **Raggles** comes alive fitfully and ineffectually, his worship of the Crawley family ensuring his ultimate imprisonment; while **Mrs Clapp** and her husband take in the Sedleys and help to sustain them with their limited means. **Miss Swartz** shows that she has a warm heart – a rare quality in Vanity Fair – as well as plenty of money. The novel opens with two minor characters of immediate impact – the Pinkerton sisters. **Miss Pinkerton**, the 'Semiramis of Hammersmith' (p. 39), is an autocratic, ignorant, snobbish woman; **Miss Jemima** is a good-natured, red-nosed creature. The interaction between she-who-must-be-obeyed and the younger sister, who feels that Becky, too, should have a Johnson's Dictionary, is keenly observed. Miss Pinkerton's humiliation by Becky shows the latter's nerve and potential. Other characters are etched – I use the word deliberately – in passing: Thackeray can capture the pathos and genuineness of Ensign Stubble, the grotesque possessiveness of General

Tufto, the slipperiness of Mr Wenham, or the kindliness of Captain Macmurdo, with superb accuracy.

But one character is certainly taken from the life – perhaps two lives – and this is **Lord Steyne**, probably based on the second and third Marquises of Hertford. The latter died in 1842, and was surrounded by scandal after his death. Thackeray gives his Steyne some factual links – his being in the Prince Regent's circle, for example, as well as his luxurious and ostentatious entertainments, his honours and the quarrels over his will. Steyne, however, dies in 1830, which marks the outer time span of the novel, and Thackeray also has him captivated by Becky and beaten by Rawdon in his fiction. Steyne gives a very positive sense of period to the novel and is representative of the upper reaches of society which Becky penetrates. He is lavish, even generous, has absorbed a great deal of culture and is tyrannical, bullying and contemptuous by turns. A sensation seeker, Lord Steyne has the requisite toadies to smooth his paths and aftermaths.

He appears somewhat mysteriously at Curzon Street, his comings and goings frequent, and at first he seems to be a grotesque in the tradition of old Sir Pitt. We are told that he 'began to grin hideously, his little eyes leering towards Rebecca' (p. 445). His physical appearance is described in detail, and he resents Becky's reference to his past, though the author observes that 'he had won his marquisate, it was said, at the gaming-table' (p. 446). He soon begins to refer to Rawdon as 'Mrs Crawley's husband' (p. 446) in order to show his contempt, and although he sees through Becky – we note that he observes she is a bad mother – he is still fascinated by her talent and her sexuality. Chapter 47 ('Gaunt House') is devoted to filling in mock-historical details of Steyne's life and inheritance (as well as contemporary references of fact to give a sense of authenticity), and his marriage to his pious wife, all of which is conveyed through the medium of 'Tom Eaves'.

On Steyne's family there is the shadow of madness, but he rules his womenfolk, and they are persuaded to write an invitation to Becky and Rawdon for their Friday dinner. Steyne shows some humanity; he realizes when the men rejoin the ladies that his wife has been friendly to Becky and he speaks to her, calling her by her Christian name. It is the only time we see him humble. He snarls – he dislikes Briggs, who is in his way – and when he acclaims Becky as Clytemnestra he does it 'between his teeth' (p. 596), because he believes that she *would* have the nerve to kill, and this excites him. After the charades he follows Becky everywhere, having already done so much for the family as to ensure their indebtedness to him. He has got little Rawdon into Whitefriars, arranges a situation for Miss Briggs, thus getting rid of the watchdog, and connives to get

Rawdon arrested for debt. Only Lady Jane's action in taking the money to Rawdon thwarts him. He is brave in the face of Rawdon's anger, but is nearly throttled and then scarred by the diamond ornament.

He cannot afford the scandal of a duel and dispatches Wenham to head off Rawdon and Macmurdo. He quickly secures the appointment of Rawdon as Governor of Coventry Island, but one wonders here if his motives aren't to get rid of the now embarrassing Becky too. They meet in passing in Rome. By now Steyne's red whiskers are dyed purple, but the scar from the diamond makes a burning red mark on his forehead, and he looks at Becky as if he has seen a ghost. Fiche tells her to leave Rome, and we feel that Steyne is quite capable of having her killed if she doesn't.

The author describes his end – 'a series of fits, brought on ... by the downfall of the ancient French Monarchy' (p. 753). It is a brilliantly satirical account, beginning with a mock-catalogue of his titles and ending with the cunningly journalistic distortion which always accompanies the death of the great, whose sins are rapidly forgotten because of the eminence of their position. But the last paragraph records the squabbles over his will, and the removal of the 'Jew's eye' diamond by Madame de Belladonna. As Geoffrey and Kathleen Tillotson rightly note, Lord Steyne supplies most of the period flavour of the novel; he is a scheming, brutal man, always conscious of position and craving for sensation, thoroughly detestable and, of course, one of the great in the world of Vanity Fair – but morally despicable in Thackeray's *Vanity Fair*.

The Teller in his Tale

As John Sutherland observes of Thackeray, 'His pre-*Vanity Fair* pen-names and assumed personae are legion'; but in his greatest work he is the greatest character and his own man. Only once in the narrative does Thackeray pretend to delegate responsibility for what he is saying, and that is when, in Chapter 47 – 'Gaunt House' – he says that all his information comes from 'little Tom Eaves' (p. 545). The choice of name, as ever with Thackeray, is significant, implying eavesdropping, here of a society nature. Another authorial device occurs in Chapter 62 – 'Am Rhein' – when he uses the first person, evocative of intimacy with the characters, and observes, 'It was at the little comfortable Ducal town of Pumpernickel ... that I first saw Colonel Dobbin and his party' (p. 721). This is a bold stroke, since Thackeray himself was in Weimar in 1830–31, so that he is in a sense putting part of his own history into the novel, which is essentially a history of its own time. Though this chapter contains some of his most obvious burlesque sketches, it serves again to convey that sense of period which is so vital an ingredient in the success and appeal of *Vanity Fair*.

Kathleen Tillotson has referred to Thackeray possessing 'the practised skill of the journalist'; to this we might add that he has a number of ventriloquial skills – these are generally associated with Dickens – and that the range of his own voice is considerable. The voice is, admittedly, that of the leisured gentleman who holds to certain moral codes and is strongly critical of certain aspects of the society he is describing. But within that area it can be that of clubman, historian, philosopher, friend, brother, sufferer, sinner and more. It is never complacent and it is never dull. That voice is the unifying adhesive of *Vanity Fair*: it comments, describes, evaluates, defends and accepts in intimate colloquy with the reader. The result is that just as the novel is about multiple personalities, so it is also about the multiplicity of personality – the author's. This gives *Vanity Fair* its unique quality; it is both microcosmic and macrocosmic at the same time.

'Before the Curtain' is important to our understanding of the author's conception, though the claim of mere puppetry is needlessly modest, since the Manager of the Performance, as he puts it, does not retire. He is ever present, commenting on his creations as he puts them into particular situations, seeing them live (or die) through those situations, and then passing on with them into new experiences. The final chapter of the novel,

'Which Contains Births, Marriages, and Deaths', shows how far the 'Manager' has come from performance to fictional reality. That reality is present from the beginning, and it is in one of the first omniscient comments in the narrative:

> All which details, I have no doubt, JONES, who reads this book at his Club, will pronounce to be excessively foolish, trivial, twaddling, and ultra-sentimental ... Well, he is a lofty man of genius, and admires the great and heroic in life and novels; and so had better take warning and go elsewhere. (pp. 43–4)

Thackeray's aim, then, is a realistic portrayal of life and not a false or idealized one. Yet if we look again at the quotation above we shall note that he is critical of himself – and people like himself – who read and comment as a way of passing life, instead of living it. The authorial irony is here directed at literature which is not concerned with the realities of living.

The modes of omniscient influence in the novel are many. The first number, as we have seen, is virtually direct narrative both in the present – Amelia and Becky arriving in Russell Square – and in the past, with retrospect on Becky and Jos. But the author's ironic conception of Becky's state leads him to pronounce on the art of arranging marriages. Becky, after all, has no mamma to whom she can entrust the 'task of husband-hunting' (p. 57), and Thackeray's appraisal of one of the most vital activities in Vanity Fair is given in a series of rhetorical questions:

> What causes young people to 'come *out*', but the noble ambition of matrimony? What sends them trooping to watering-places? What keeps them dancing till five o'clock in the morning through a whole mortal season? What causes them to labour at pianoforte sonatas, and to learn four songs from a fashionable master at a guinea a lesson ... (p. 57)

We shall hear this voice often in *Vanity Fair*, for it is both satirical and ironic of other current practices. '

Thus we get the occasional aside to the reader in which we learn something of the author's own views – for example, on music. Becky sings a number 'of those simple ballads which were the fashion forty years ago' (p. 72), and this gives the author occasion to reveal his own tastes: ,

> They are not, it is said, very brilliant, in a musical point of view, but contain numberless good-natured, simple appeals to the affections, which people understood better than the milk-and-water *lagrime*, *sospiri*, and *felicità* of the eternal Donizettian music with which we are favoured now-a-days. (p. 73)

This does not impede the narrative flow, but it brings us closer to the writer. It is not confiding so much as thrown in casually as Becky is about to sing a sentimental ballad relative to her own case – and cause – which

will appeal to the sentimental Jos, and increase the chances of his proposing to her. The author has already measured that appeal 'to the
affections' in the case of the 'simple' Jos.

Sometimes Thackeray strikes a poignant note when he reveals something of his own past, perhaps in the form of a generalization, perhaps
directly personal. Thus Thackeray the man as well as author, again using
one of his favourite modes – the rhetorical question – identifies himself
and the reader with the loneliness of the boy Dobbin, who has been put
in his place by George Osborne and passes a half-holiday 'in the bitterest
sadness and woe. Who amongst us is there that does not recollect similar
hours of bitter, bitter childish grief?' (p. 77). This passes to an indictment
of the system which we know that Thackeray himself had endured – 'and
how many of those gentle souls do you degrade, estrange, torture, for the
sake of a little loose arithmetic, and miserable dog-Latin' (p. 77). The
fictional and the personal are brought into line with the radical, for
Thackeray is a realist in his appraisal of fact, and does not hesitate,
sometimes with superb economy, to state it. Thus we find Cuff's caning
of George Osborne accompanied by the Thackerayan comment, 'Torture
in a public school is as much licensed as the knout in Russia' (p. 80).

The fight between Dobbin and Cuff provides Thackeray with the
opportunity to use his mock-heroic hyperbole to good effect – 'If I had
the pen of a Napier, or a Bell's Life ... It was the last charge of the Guard
– (that is, it *would* have been, only Waterloo had not yet taken place) –
it was Ney's column ...' (p. 82). Here we note the humour, but, more
importantly, what I called earlier the unifying adhesive. A fight between
two boys is compared to what is going to be the major event of the novel,
with the author establishing an ironic perspective between past and
future. It enables him, too, to refer to a major historian (Napier) in the
same sentence as a sporting newspaper. By a subtle implication – and this
again indicates the depth to be found in Thackeray – the boys' fight is
as ephemeral as the report of a boxing match (later Captain Macmurdo
reads Bell's Life), whereas the real history of *Vanity Fair* is the task of the
author, and thus comparable to an official history. But there is also self-
mockery in the deliberately half-forgetful 'only Waterloo had not yet
taken place'.

The Vauxhall chapter (6) opens with a studied authorial statement
which defines Thackeray's method in the novel: 'I know that the tune I
am piping is a very mild one (although there are some terrific chapters
coming presently), and must beg the good-natured reader to remember
...' (p. 87). What the author is saying is that the flow of narrative – like
the flow of life – is of necessity uneven in interest. He goes on to satirize,
and parody (parody is Thackeray's real element) the modes of fiction in

which he *could* have told his story – 'We might have treated this subject in the genteel, or in the romantic, or in the facetious manner . . .' (p. 88). He then proceeds to briefly do so, thus injecting another dimension of humour into his novel, and again emphasizing his concern with realistic treatment. In the first edition of *Vanity Fair* the satirical attacks on his contemporaries were made longer by a parody near the beginning of Chapter 6, called 'The Night Attack', which opens with a storm sequence, a commonplace of sensational 'Newgate' fiction. But this was cut from the 1853 edition, Thackeray probably feeling that the objects of his satire were no longer relevant. He may even have responded to criticism from Dickens and others that such parodies 'do no honour to literature or literary men'. Whether they do or not, the reader is referred to page 88 for the sheer verve and fun with which Thackeray castigates the ephemeral novelistic modes of his time, as he attempts to give permanence to his own.

The Vauxhall chapter is further enhanced by the author's use of fate or coincidence, here seen in Jos's consumption of most of the bowl of rack punch. The commentary before it establishes once more the sense of perspective essential to Thackeray's method in *Vanity Fair*, here with the additional evidence of analogies with Fair Rosamond and Alexander the Great:

> So did this bowl of rack punch influence the fates of all the principal characters in this 'Novel without a Hero', which we are now relating. It influenced their life, although most of them did not taste a drop of it. (p. 93)

Again the author's tone is ironic, but later he uses his own (supposed) experience to reinforce the narrative impact of what Jos has done:

> What is the rack in the punch, at night, to the rack in the head of a morning? To this truth I can vouch as a man; there is no headache in the world like that caused by Vauxhall punch. Through the lapse of twenty years I can remember the consequences of two glasses! – two wine glasses! (p. 95)

The narrator, then, has been subject to human frailty, but in moderation, while Jos of course has indulged himself to excess. The tone is endearing, confiding, both the reader and writer enjoying the joke. This is part of what I would call the charm of *Vanity Fair*. The word 'charm' sometimes carries with it the derogatory implication of superficiality and lightness; but I feel that Thackeray's charm lies in the fact that he woos his reader in different voices, and that many of those voices charm the reader into a recognition of shared experience. We sense the man behind the voice, respond to his amusement, criticism or tolerance, whatever it may be.

Another aspect of the authorial voice is its occasional nostalgic reminiscence. A good example occurs in Chapter 7, when Becky is on her way to Queen's Crawley and the author bemoans the loss of the coaches. It is movingly set in context – and has some affiliations with George Eliot's introduction to *Felix Holt the Radical* – but the personal tone, the genuine sense of regret, are what come across to the reader:

> But the writer of these pages, who has pursued in former days, and in the same bright weather, the same remarkable journey, cannot but think of it with a sweet and tender regret. (p. 108)

In Thackeray, as in George Eliot and Dickens, we always obtain a strong sense of the past, of traditions which have departed and whose loss is felt in the present. The notes of intimacy strike a responsive chord in the reader, who looks forward to them. They are not interruptions so much as extensions; after Becky's first letter to Amelia, the author feels moved to comment on Becky as a 'droll funny creature' and to make his own position as author clear to his readers, in whom he has already confided a number of times. Clearly the emphasis is on truth to life:

> And while the moralist, who is holding forth on the cover (an accurate portrait of your humble servant), professes to wear neither gown nor bands, but only the very same long-eared livery in which his congregation is arrayed: yet, look you, one is bound to speak the truth as far as one knows it, whether one mounts a cap and bells or a shovel-hat; and a deal of disagreeable matter must come out in the course of such an undertaking. (p. 116)

Those who accuse Thackeray of cynicism should study the above passage which, despite its humour, is intent on establishing that the writer is the same as his reader – in that they both partake of humanity, and that the responsibility of that writer is to 'speak the truth'. This is an oblique, but certainly serious way of elevating the stature and practice of the novelist at the expense of the romantic and the sensational forms. At the same time, the use of the word 'moralist' shows that Thackeray considers himself required by the nature of his profession to express moral views or present moral situations. The latter are, of course, the substance of *Vanity Fair*, and the money needed for social advancement, ostentation or living well on nothing a year is constantly in Thackeray's mind. With Miss Crawley's command of her servants and relations, and always aware of her importance in the plot of his novel, the author affects to laugh at himself for being the same as everyone else in playing for a legacy. He mocks all servility to such thought of gain:

> Ah, gracious powers! I wish you would send me an old aunt – a maiden aunt – an aunt with a lozenge on her carriage, and a front of light coffee-coloured hair – how my children should work workbags for her, and my Julia and I would make her comfortable! Sweet – sweet vision! Foolish – foolish dream! (pp. 124–5)

We should note the last phrases carefully, for they are a moral comment on all aspects of self-gain and self-interest. Thackeray sees into the motivations of human nature, indeed possesses them himself, and has the maturity to recognize them for what they are.

His maturity and wisdom, in print if not in practice, are everywhere evident in *Vanity Fair*. The attentive reader will notice how frequently he refers to the title of his novel *in his own voice* to emphasize the moral arc he is tracing through his characters. That moral arc is nowhere better in evidence than in his presentation of Amelia – the omniscient voice here being deployed to balance the gossip in the novel, and even to forestall his own critics who found Amelia insipid. The opening of Chapter 12 has Thackeray conducting an argument in which he says that 'It is quite edifying to hear women speculate upon the worthlessness and the duration of beauty' (p. 146) and concluding, 'I am tempted to think that to be despised by her sex is a very great compliment to a woman' (p. 147). This is all a prelude to the Misses Osbornes' treatment of Amelia, and it serves to underline the jealousies and vanities which mar lives.

One feels that the author is here adopting a conventional male attitude, which is one of protectiveness towards someone as timid, quiet, withdrawn and yet attractive as Amelia. But I suggest that the emphasis is much more than a merely male, chauvinistic stance. The use of the author's voice deliberately registers unkindness and superficiality where none is merited. Thackeray is saying that we judge by appearances, are jealous of beauty (this is where the chauvinism comes in, for George's brother officers, for example, are not jealous of him) and that we do not trouble to look beneath the surface.

All this is in the direct context of the wider Vanity Fair, which judges people not for what they are in reality, but for what they appear to be – in Becky's case artless and innocent, in Steyne's the possession of a pedigree which establishes him as one of the aristocratic elite. In both cases the world and its judgements, its moral standards, are wrong; Becky is an artful, scheming, unscrupulous and prostituted woman; Steyne is a decadent, degraded, corrupt 'Wicked Nobleman ... which Old Nick will fetch away at the end of this singular performance' (p. 34). Thus early in his novel Thackeray is preparing the reader for the distinction between those who inflict suffering and those who innocently suffer. Nothing is more offensive than virtue in Vanity Fair – Amelia suffers early on from a surfeit of it, and we know how Lady Jane's caused Becky to hate her. Amelia's coming poverty causes Thackeray to satirize marriages for money, such as that between Lord Methuselah and Miss Trotter.

The author's acknowledged dislike of George Osborne leads him to reinforce the presentation of his character with authorial observations like, 'Some cynical Frenchman has said that there are two parties to a love transaction: the one who loves, and the other who condescends to be so treated' (p. 159). That this is meant to be definitive of George and Amelia there is no doubt, and perhaps the irony of this reference is that it continues beyond death and ruins life. But Thackeray is also master of the grotesque as well as of the distasteful, and enjoys jokes at the expense of those of his readers who form expectations of what will happen in the next number. Thus at the end of Chapter 14 we have Sir Pitt Crawley on his knees proposing to Becky. Thackeray opens Chapter 15 (the beginning of the fifth number) with a wonderfully satirical glance back at what he has done, and a glance across at the expectant reader:

> Every reader of a sentimental turn (and we desire no other) must have been pleased with the *tableau* with which the last act of our little drama concluded; for what can be prettier than an image of Love on his knees before Beauty? (p. 186)

This is a parody of a proposal, for Sir Pitt is physically hideous and Becky spiritually corrupt. The personifications of Love and Beauty, the reference to the 'act' and the 'drama', show Thackeray mocking the sentimental novel of romance by undercutting it with his irony. In fact, it *is* an act of a drama, for Becky is always acting and Sir Pitt is a caricature of a suitor. But the subtlest irony lies in the opening remark, since Thackeray realizes that 'acts' of this sort are going to capture the kind of reader who would not perhaps normally be drawn towards *Vanity Fair*. Sir Pitt *is* a baronet; we are nominally in *high society*, where romantic proposals are a commonplace, at least in fiction. Shortly afterwards he is parodying an extension of this kind of romance – the snobbery of aristocratic pretensions. Becky, already married to Rawdon in secret, realizes that she might have been the wife of a baronet instead of just hoping that Rawdon will get Miss Crawley's money.

The social climbing which characterizes Vanity Fair is given ironic appraisal, when the author tells how he was 'in the Fair myself, at an evening party' (p. 193). There he sees Miss Toady paying attention to Mrs Briefless, and is later told the reason for it:

> 'You know,' she said, 'Mrs Briefless is granddaughter of Sir John Redhand, who is so ill at Cheltenham that he can't last six months. Mrs Briefless's papa succeeds; so you see she *will* be a baronet's daughter.' (p. 193)

Ironically, Becky is to find herself related to a baronet, and gets herself presented at Court as she wishes. It is perhaps the highest aim in Vanity Fair.

The lowest rung of the social ladder is also encompassed by the omniscient voice, and Thackeray cunningly gets in a topical reference which would certainly be recognized by his readers in 1847. The fall of the Sedleys is chronicled obliquely in the introduction to Chapter 17. Thackeray is still laughing at novel-readers, pushing his own method but, in essence, presenting success and failure in Vanity Fair:

If there is any exhibition in all Vanity Fair which Satire and Sentiment can visit arm in arm together; where you light on the strangest contrasts, laughable and tearful: where you may be gentle and pathetic, or savage and cynical with perfect propriety: It is at one of those public assemblies, a crowd of which are advertised every day in the last page of the *Times* newspaper, and over which the late Mr George Robins used to preside with so much dignity. (p. 204)

This is the auction sale – George Robins, a celebrated auctioneer, had died early in 1847 – of the Sedleys' property, at which satire and sentiment do indeed go hand in hand.

Here Thackeray combines the contemporary reference in life with the functional reference in his fiction. Becky and Rawdon are to buy the picture of Jos seated on an elephant, which Becky is later to show Jos, and thus inveigle him into believing that she has always loved him. Dobbin is to buy the piano which Amelia believes for years has come from George – that present forming, or helping to form, the major part of her delusion. The contrasts referred to by the author are the contrasts which run throughout the novel and throughout life – those of success and failure which produce sincerity and loyalty, as in Dobbin; opportunism and laughter, as in Becky and Rawdon. Again the authorial assertion is precisely linked to the plot.

Another aspect of such linking is that of the broadly historical with the individual. Sedley's fortunes are bound up with the re-emergence of Napoleon. Thackeray opens Chapter 18 – again a retrospect to explain the collapse of John Sedley's fortune – with a modest disclaimer which is in itself a comment on the influence of the great upon the small:

Our surprised story now finds itself for a moment among very famous events and personages, and hanging on the skirts of history. When the eagles of Napoleon Bonaparte, the Corsican upstart ... *Bon Dieu,* I say, is it not hard that the fateful rush of the great Imperial struggle can't take place without affecting a poor harmless girl of eighteen ... (pp. 213–14)

Vanity Fair is a historical novel in the true sense of the definition, for the tide of history, the influence of large events on individuals, is integral to its own movement. The perspective in the above quotation is one which the author maintains throughout the novel with, admittedly, Waterloo and its repercussions the pivot on which the action turns. But Thackeray's interjections, like the one above, though seemingly casual are in fact weighted with a compassionate irony and structural awareness which is peculiarly his own.

Napoleon's hundred days change the course of the lives we are watching develop, and we should note that the authorial persona refers to his story as 'hanging on the skirts of history' – a modest distancing which he is later to practise in the Waterloo chapters. The lightness which characterizes his touch – his feeling for period and for contemporary humour – is seen in the *'Bon Dieu'*. The most common of French expressions, it is in keeping, perhaps, with the rise of the 'upstart'. But the subtlest part of this introduction is the reference to Amelia who, later (and this is where the foreshadowing irony comes in), is to be more than affected by 'the great Imperial struggle'. She is to become distracted, and the implication is that history changes lives, and that if it is our fate to be born at a particular time, the events of that time will condition our lives. This historical consciousness is examined in the Appendix to this study, but we may note here that the author's use of a voice in historical perspective is perhaps one of the major unifying adhesives in the text.

At times the authorial comments on marriage, with their attendant financial implications, are frankly cynical, though the confiding tone remains. Take, for example, this address to the reader, and consider it in the light of the marriages in the novel:

> Be cautious, then, young ladies; be wary how you engage. Be shy of loving frankly; never tell all you feel or (a better way still), feel very little. See the consequences of being prematurely honest and confiding, and mistrust yourselves and everybody. Get yourselves married as they do in France, where the lawyers are the bridesmaids and the confidantes ... That is the way to get on, and be respected, and have a virtuous character in Vanity Fair. (p. 220)

Apart from Amelia, and the infatuated Rawdon, is there a marriage for love in the novel? Dobbin's love is wasted, Lady Jane's marriage to Pitt is arranged and, though we might ponder on Peggy O'Dowd's marriage, there is insufficient evidence that she really belongs to Vanity Fair anyway. When Sedley confesses their ruin to his wife there is a keen insight into that early love which is rekindled at this moment of crisis; but we note that this early love was before they began to live in Vanity Fair. Again, the seeming casualness of tone – the friendly address – belies the seriousness of the intention. In displaying Vanity Fair for us, Thackeray is demonstrating its negation of human qualities; purse and rank rule, at the expense of love and kindness. Although he says that 'it is only a comedy that the reader pays his money to witness' (p. 229), we are under no illusions that the comedy of marriage in society is a sick one.

Thackeray's constant reference to his title is the reason for my frequent allusion to it here. He never lets the reader escape from its consequences, identifying his reader's life with the lives of his characters. I have quoted at length in this section to show the main areas of authorial control and the varying personae used by Thackeray in moral, historical and contemporary reflection, but I am mindful of Lady Eastlake's observation that:

> It is impossible to quote from his book with any justice to it. The whole growth of the narrative is so matted and interwoven together with tendril-like links and bindings, that there is no detaching a flower with sufficient length of stalk to exhibit it to advantage.

If the final part of this analogy is clumsy or strained, it is nonetheless true, and in the remainder of this section I intend to draw the reader's attention to sections of the novel, the detailed study of which will reinforce, or even extend, what has gone before.

There is a fine ironic section on the influence of the past – which is not nostalgic, but destructive – where the embarrassments, the changes, the recollections of 'Vows, love, promises, confidences, gratitude, how queerly they read after a while! There ought to be a law in Vanity Fair ordering the destruction of every written document (except receipted tradesmen's bills) after a certain brief and proper interval' (p. 231). How tellingly this contrasts with Miss Matty's looking through the old letters of her parents in *Cranford* (1851–3), and how *true* is Thackeray's appraisal by comparison. Sometimes that truth to life is undermined, however, by the exigencies of the plot. Once again the opening of a chapter (here 23) is used to promote the qualities of friendship as exemplified by Dobbin's activities on George's behalf:

> What is the secret mesmerism which friendship possesses, and under the operation of which a person ordinarily sluggish, or cold, or timid, becomes wise, active, and resolute, in another's behalf? (p. 266)

This is the prelude to Dobbin's attempt to win old Sedley and old Osborne over in the question of George's marriage to Amelia, and we note that the language, apart from words like 'active' and 'resolute', does not fit Dobbin at all. It is one of the rare instances of slackness in Thackeray's writing. On his own modes of narration, however, he is explicit, for there is more than just a passing truth in his 'Our history is destined in this chapter to go backwards and forwards in a very irresolute manner seemingly' (p. 293). It is a modest disclaimer of his own organization in *Vanity Fair*, but also definitive of a sophisticated structural cohesion; not merely applicable to this chapter but to many, where the events of the past condition and form the present. Character is its own history and Thackeray's 'history', as we have seen, is personal, local and national.

Perhaps the most signal instance in *Vanity Fair* of the author taking a particular perspective and keeping to it with cumulative dramatic effects (apart from one brief telling departure to which I shall refer later) is his statement at the beginning of Chapter 30, in the Waterloo sequence:

> We do not claim to rank among the military novelists. Our place is with the non-combatants. When the decks are cleared for action we go below and wait meekly. We should only be in the way of the manoeuvres that the gallant fellows are performing overhead. (p. 346)

This is all the more remarkable since Thackeray had given some time, as we know, to a study of G. R. Gleig's *The Story of the Battle of Waterloo* (1847); though admittedly that historian refers to the number of non-combatants, even wives and children, who were taken to the Low Countries prior to the battle. The gain in narrative impact which follows this statement is telling indeed, for the preparations described by Thackeray enable him to use a series of contrasts – Amelia and George, Becky and Rawdon, the O'Dowds, Jos – to create an atmosphere of tension, fear, uncertainty and near hysteria.

In the best journalistic fashion he is also able to deploy first one rumour then another, as well as balancing the humorous scene between Jos and Isidor with the dramatic arrival of young Ensign Stubble, wounded, but with optimistic news of George – news which even more dramatically proves to be fallacious in the sequel. Only on the last page of Chapter 32 does Thackeray forsake his self-imposed meekness and then, with superb economy, devotes one long paragraph to the final stage of the battle, followed by one short paragraph reporting the death of George. But there is nothing meek about his assertion of the futility of war and what it breeds: the voice of the humane Thackeray is heard loud and clear when he remarks:

> ... there is no end to the so-called glory and shame, and to the alternations of successful and unsuccessful murder, in which two high-spirited nations might engage. Centuries hence, we Frenchmen and Englishmen might be boasting and killing each other still, carrying out bravely the Devil's code of honour. (p. 385)

It is this kind of statement which gives *Vanity Fair* its relevance for all time, and it shows Thackeray transcending the narrow confines of patriotism in his abiding love for humanity.

Some of the most brilliantly satirical barbs are saved for Vanity Fair at peace, seen in Chapter 36 – 'How to Live Well on Nothing a Year' – where the author uses his own supposed experiences with friends to give credibility to the swindling initiated by Becky on her arrival in Curzon Street. He follows this in the next chapter by explaining, 'we are bound to describe how a house may be got for nothing a year' (p. 435). The 'bound to' strikes the right moral and realistic tone, because it suggests that the truth will not be eroded by any social considerations. The probing of that truth leads to other practical speculations, such as how many people are ruined by others, and Thackeray here examines – in his own voice – the injustice which makes one law for the rich and another for the poor. He points out that the bankrupt nobleman who flees abroad wins respect for the vastness of his ruin, and he asks, 'who pities a poor barber who can't get his money for powdering the footman's heads' (p. 438).

This considered social and moral comment underlines the views of critics like Barbara Hardy, who see Thackeray the novelist as profoundly radical in his criticism of the upper reaches of a society whose corruption brings misery, poverty and imprisonment for the less fortunate. He extends his satire to embrace the exclusiveness of this society which initially rejects Becky, though he qualifies this with a typically witty aside – 'With regard to the world of female fashion and its customs, the present writer of course can only speak at second-hand' (p. 440). He further expatiates on the fact that attractive women inevitably have themselves accompanied by a plain companion when they are seen in public, and uses this to underline the contrast with Amelia and her small domestic duties, which he describes ironically as 'but trivial incidents to recount in the life of our heroine' (p. 460). The irony is that these duties consist of caring for her child in deprived circumstances, very distinct from Becky's social display, when she appears to her child 'like a vivified figure out of the *Magasin des Modes*' (p. 448).

The satire of society is extended to the death of that 'old Silenus', Sir Pitt, where Thackeray is moved to another moral comment when he observes that if any of us could come back from beyond the grave 'I suppose he or she (assuming that any Vanity Fair feelings subsist in the sphere whither we are bound) would have a pang of mortification at finding how soon our survivors are consoled' (p. 493). There is a general but by no means universal truth in this; however, it is peculiarly appropriate to the unlamented Sir Pitt.

As the novel advances, so the moral tone deepens, particularly with regard to Becky. But the pronouncements are still general, and may often be taken as indicating Thackeray's deeply held beliefs about people, hence the charge of cynicism:

> . . . for my part I believe that remorse is the least active of all a man's moral senses – the very easiest to be deadened when wakened: and in some never wakened at all.
>
> We grieve at being found out, and at the idea of shame or punishment; but the mere sense of wrong makes very few people unhappy in Vanity Fair. (p. 497)

Again the context for this pronouncement is absolutely right; Becky has a momentary urge for the country life, nostalgic about her last stay at Queen's Crawley seven years previously, but finally rejects what Thackeray calls being 'honest and humble' (p. 497) because she is 'committed to the other path' (p. 497). Remorse never enters Becky's soul, her sense of wrong is non-existent and any grief she feels at being found out is quickly submerged in the next round of manipulative activity.

Sometimes the authorial pronouncement can be subtracted from the larger example being given, and convey a freshness of truth or wisdom. Thackeray is not, essentially, a writer whose work is littered with proverbialisms (though there are some), since his confiding addresses are usually given at some length. But he does sometimes achieve an admirable compression, as in 'To part with money is a sacrifice beyond almost all men endowed with a sense of order' (p. 520), where he is considering Sir Pitt's inheritance from Miss Crawley at the expense of Rawdon and his needs. Nuggets like these are found throughout the novel, but the teller sometimes ranges far beyond two or three paragraphs.

At the beginning of this chapter I mentioned Thackeray's introduction of a character/narrator called Tom Eaves, who fills in all the necessary detail on Gaunt House and the history of Lord Steyne's family in Chapter 47. In a sense, Thackeray enjoys the joke he is having with the reader, placing the responsibility for anything spicy or scandalous on a fictitious narrator, in order to retain a distance from that responsibility. It is a cunning device which he confines to brackets in order to provide an unhindered continuity – '(little Tom Eaves, who knows everything, and who showed me the place)' (p. 545) – and allowing the author to make a number of references of a gossipy but historical nature, such as that to 'The Prince and Perdita' (p. 545), in reality George IV and one of his mistresses who had died in 1800.

Set beside his general account of the Steyne history runs the Eavesian account of the family, including the humiliations of Lady Steyne at the hands of her debauched husband. If this were all the joke would be funny; however, there is more, and it consists of making Tom Eaves, in his lowly position, one of the toadies of Vanity Fair. He 'knows everybody's affairs' (p. 546), he comments on the great ladies (Thackeray says he would have gladly sacrificed his wife to get a bow from any of them), affects of course to disapprove of them, and advantageously compares the lot of the poor man with the great. The whole narrative here is profoundly satirical – 'always according to Mr Eaves' (p. 548) – but the masterstroke is to come. Having condemned the great, we are told:

And here, haply, a great man coming up, Tom Eaves's hat would drop off his head, and he would rush forward with a bow and a grin, which showed that he knew the world too – in the Tomeavesian way, that is. (p. 549)

It is the great levelling remark; the perspective is redressed, for we are all part of Vanity Fair whoever we are, and subscribe to its standards however much we may criticize them.

Becky's Court presentation comes in for some authorial satire in a parody of high journalism. It begins, 'We are authorized to state that Mrs Rawdon Crawley's *costume de cour . . .*' (p. 556), but gives way to another kind of satire which embraces the whole social grotesquerie of such presentations of elderly, but elaborately made-up members of the aristocracy. The author recommends the absence of strong light:

> Drawing-rooms should be announced for November, or the first foggy day: or the elderly sultanas of our Vanity Fair should drive up in closed litters, descend in a covered way and make their curtsey to the Sovereign under the protection of lamplight. (p. 557)

The presentation of Becky herself is discreetly and reticently passed over in a hushed authorial aside ('Loyal respect and decency tell even the imagination not to look too keenly and audaciously about the sacred audience chamber . . .' (p. 560)), but the language is an effective mockery of the scene – another radical shaft not only at the 'August Presence', but also at the meaningless pomp and display by which so many set so much store.

Occasionally, in true mock-heroic style, Thackeray will invoke 'The Muse, whoever she be, who presides over this Comic History . . .' (p. 574), but he can also draw analogies which underline the fact that everything is transitory including, of course, Becky's triumph. The reticence, which we have noted above, is very much part of Thackeray's authorial stance as Becky goes to Gaunt House for her last major success – the charades. Yet once more there is a duality about it. When he says, 'an uninitiated man cannot take upon himself to portray the great world accurately, and had best keep his opinions to himself whatever they are' (p. 587), he is virtually duping the reader into thinking he has little to say. In fact the charades are described in great detail, since they are part of the symbolic chain of unity. For instance, the penultimate Thackerayan illustration in the first edition of *Vanity Fair* is called, 'Becky's second appearance in the character of Clytemnestra'. It shows her standing behind the curtain while Dobbin talks to an abject Jos. The implication is that she will kill Jos, and there are dark hints that she eventually does, or at least drives him to his death. In the second charade Becky had played the part of Clytemnestra, killing Rawdon as Agamemnon symbolically onstage, while her offstage activities – almost certainly conspiring with Steyne to have her husband arrested for debt – effectively kill their marriage. The reticent voice, while disclaiming to do so, has effectively described events in 'the great world accurately'. It is quite typical of Thackeray's relationship with his readers that he should indulge his private joke in this sardonic manner. It further illustrates the depth at which he works.

Sometimes, however, Thackeray does tell us what he is *not* going to do, in order to subserve the structure of his novel. Steyne having arranged little Rawdon's future at Whitefriars, Thackeray resists what must have been something of a temptation. He says, 'Our business does not lie with the second generation and Master Rawdon's life at school, otherwise the present tale might be carried to any indefinite length' (p. 606), and thus prepares us for the rounding off at the end of the novel. His firm grasp of narrative tension here brings us back to Rawdon's rescue by Lady Jane, with its immediate and dramatic results and repercussions. Authorial comments decrease in density as the various strands of *Vanity Fair* are carefully knitted together. Amelia's acceptance of Mr Osborne's bounty does call forth a moral comment on the unevenness of wealth – 'that lottery of life which gives to this man the purple and fine linen, and sends to the other rags for garments and dogs for comforters' (p. 662) – and there is an even stronger moral injunction to the reader to 'be humble, my brother, in your prosperity! Be gentle with those who are less lucky, if not more deserving' (p. 663). These comments are of a piece with the running humanity in Thackeray's appraisal of the fictional inhabitants of *Vanity Fair*.

The intimacy which the author has established with his readers is exemplified in the Pumpernickel episode, where Thackeray is undoubtedly drawing satirically on his own experiences in Weimar. Here he speaks of meeting 'Colonel Dobbin and his party' (p. 721), but then shifts the emphasis from 'I' to 'We'. The effect is that of interested, companionable exchanges, with the teller in his tale becoming an unidentified character in it: 'We watched them, too, out of the theatre ... We all walked together ... We rather hoped that nice-looking woman would be induced to stay some time in the town' (pp. 724–5). It is warmly effective, bringing an immediacy to the narrative, and perhaps reminding us that 'Before the Curtain' – Thackeray's preface to the novel when it was issued in book form in June 1848 – contains the puppet analogy which did not occur to him until he had nearly completed *Vanity Fair* in its monthly issues. 'The Manager' and his 'puppets' were virtually an afterthought and, as has been pointed out by John Sutherland, the preface 'is properly speaking an epilogue'.

The presence of the narrator 'Am Rhein' adds to the realism which I have stressed throughout this book. It is a natural extension, not merely of the presence of the author in the novel, but also of his clever use of yet another voice, here from within the action, so to speak. It is continued in the next chapter, before Becky dramatically reappears, with some finely ironic descriptions of the various aspects of Pumpernickel, carrying particular emphasis both on ostentation and imitation, and with some passing glances at its constitution, which 'is or was a moderate despotism, tempered by a Chamber that might or might not be elected. I never certainly could hear of its sitting in my time at Pumpernickel' (p. 729).

The retrospect on Becky (Chapter 64) opens with yet another ironic 'We', but it is the authorial 'we' rather than that of character intimacy:

> We must pass over a part of Mrs Rebecca Crawley's biography with that lightness and delicacy which the world demands – the moral world, that has, perhaps, no particular objection to vice, but an insuperable repugnance to hearing vice called by its proper name. (p. 737)

It is a neat indictment of hypocrisy, and is brilliantly followed up by the remark that no 'truly refined English or American female will permit the word breeches to be pronounced in her chaste hearing' (p. 737). Here, as elsewhere in the novel, Thackeray's wit is displayed to advantage.

As we have already seen, Thackeray's voices are various, but always they enrich and enhance the novel, and stimulate the reader. We are aware of the man behind the mask, of a vast and radiating wisdom, tolerance and humanity, which embrace the spectrum of human experience. Some critics have found the author's presence in the novel intrusive, as if the readers are being lectured. There are, however, no lectures or homilies in *Vanity Fair*. The voice is never strident with propaganda or smooth with insinuation. It is intimate or rhetorical, kind or critical, imbued with a moral, social, philosophical or historical perspective, but always vital and compelling. Its mimicry captures the tones of life, in which comedy and tragedy coexist in all the plans and uncertainties of individuals and societies. The personality of the teller permeates every corner of his tale, and we are the richer for the experience.

Style and Structure

In his excellent book on *The Language of Thackeray* (1978), K. C. Phillipps quotes James Hannay's astute definition of Thackeray's 'gentlemanly tone' as managing to 'hit the right mean between a bookishness which is too stiff and a colloquialism which is too loose'. Those words were written in 1869, six years after Thackeray's death, yet they encapsulate his manner in *Vanity Fair* and most of his other writings. In other sections of this commentary I have referred to Thackeray's modes of narration with regard to character as well as indicating the major facets of his omniscient control. Here I intend to concentrate on the main elements of what is usefully categorized as style; though with Thackeray this takes on many varieties of expression, many nuances which emphasize, by subtle implications, his own attitudes towards the society he is describing.

The word 'bookishness' does not reflect his variety of reference or, more importantly, his relaxed manner; for 'bookishness' smells somewhat of the lamp whereas *Vanity Fair* is redolent of life. We are aware, as we move through the experience of *Vanity Fair*, of Thackeray's wide reading, from the Bible and the classics to that of his own contemporaries. His scattering of literary allusions reflects his learning, but it is a learning worn lightly. A look at the early chapters shows the range of the allusions – from the Hammersmith Semiramis (Miss Pinkerton); Mrs Chapone, author of a ponderous series of letters on 'the improvement of the mind'; a standard textbook on geography by William Guthrie; a reference to the *Arabian Nights*; the historian William Napier and to Fénelon's *Télémaque*.

Shakespearean echoes are frequent; Dickens gets an oblique mention through 'old Weller' of *Pickwick Papers* and Becky cites Mrs Radcliffe's celebrated Gothic novel, *The Mysteries of Udolpho* (1794), which was undoubtedly secret extra-curricular reading for the girls of Miss Pinkerton's academy. The reference to Camilla scouring the plains (p. 127) is from the *Aeneid*, Book XI (and to Pope's *Essay on Criticism* – 'Not so when swift Camilla scours the plain'). Other references to the classics, frequently unobtrusive, are taken from Horace, while the Bible furnishes, among other things, Amelia with an Eli instead of a Samuel (p. 651) – an error not corrected until 1898.

The above is merely an indication of his range, but accompanying this, and essential to Thackeray's creation of a double time-scheme – that of nis own period and the period 1813–30 – are a number of contemporary references in each time-scale. The primary aim is undoubtedly that of authenticity and, secondly, a kind of private relationship with his reader, for nothing is as satisfying as recognizing an allusion. Again we can return to the early chapters for evidence of period reference. In the first chapter there are mentions of Mrs Billington, the opera singer who had been performing until recently (1811); the French dancers Hillisberg and Parisot; Mr Lawrence, later President of the Royal Academy (1820) in Chapter 2; Exeter Change (demolished 1829) in Chapter 4, while the celebrated actors Kean and Kemble both get a passing mention in Chapter 5. The Vauxhall chapter (6) contains an anachronism noted by the Tillotsons in their edition of *Vanity Fair*. This is the mention of Madame Saqui (p. 91), who did not appear at Vauxhall until 1816, after the fictional visit which costs Becky a proposal from Jos. Of the topical references there is one to a style of playing in 'the Herz-manner' (p. 146), while in Chapter 17 Thackeray speaks of the 'late Mr George Robins', who was, as we have seen, an auctioneer who died in 1847 – the year in which *Vanity Fair* was issued in monthly numbers. Even the mention of Alexis Soyer (p. 226), chef at the Reform Club in Thackeray's time, would have its piquancy for contemporary readers. I have given the merest selection here, but the text is abundantly strewn with this kind of almost casual reference, which makes one aware of the historical setting and the present in which Thackeray wrote. Many of the references have a satirical or ironic intention, and some will therefore be mentioned in their particular contexts later in this section.

Linked with the sense of time in *Vanity Fair* is the purely verbal style, admirably covered by Kenneth Phillipps in his book on Thackeray's language. He says, 'Thackeray has a sure touch with obsolescent and archaic language' (p. 42), and it is this which particularly conveys the Regency atmosphere which he so adeptly re-creates. Phillipps points to such words as 'character' (reputation), 'intelligence' (mutual understanding) and 'remark' (notice), as well as 'admire' (wonder at), to show how the novelist has his characters use words as they would have been used in the period. He also refers to habits as well as usage, noting the 'rout cakes' (p. 62) which Jos manages to consume, has old Osborne use the word 'younkers', while Thackeray also tells us that Amelia crossed her letters – that is, she wrote in the margins sideways and all over the page, not just straight down it. When we are told that Jos sang and made love, we have to note the deliberately dated use of the latter: Thackeray is employing 'made love' in an almost unsexual sense (convention would not allow him to be blunt, anyway), and despite the satire, the term then meant merely talking of love, perhaps 'courting' Becky with his words. This is all unobtrusive stylistically: Thackeray looked back carefully, and thoroughly observed his own society, adapting his language to both periods with a meticulous sense of accuracy and appropriateness.

We might usefully consider, having noted the period references, how Thackeray's style easily embraces a number of social areas. Though we can accept P. J. Keating's broad statement that Thackeray's writings are 'based on feelings of class or educational superiority', we again note the range, for example, of his handling of colloquial speech and dialect. Sir Pitt uses 'ship' for 'sheep' and 'zatusfy' for 'satisfy', among other apparently Hampshire derivations; while one of Thackeray's favourite areas of language is obviously to be found in the wonderful fluency of Peggy O'Dowd. Here she is in full flow:

'Sure, I couldn't stop till tay-time. Present me, Garge, my dear fellow, to your lady. Madam, I'm deloighted to see ye; and to present to you me husband, Meejor O'Dowd.' (p. 317)

Thus Auralia Margaretta; but what is clever about this is that it is not straight parody. It is a mixture of the brogue – her inheritance – with a kind of conformity. Notice that Peggy uses, for example, 'ye' and 'you', 'my' and 'me', a subtle indication that, like most of us, she uses two registers, those of natural and acquired speech. She is, to appropriate Kipling's phrase, both the Colonel's lady and Judy O'Grady under her own linguistic skin.

Rawdon has his own kind of army affectation, but the commonest use in Thackeray is that of the cockney dialect to emphasize his upstairs-downstairs distinctions. Jos's valet, who calls George 'Mr Hosbin', tells the latter that 'The Capting was obliged to bring him upstairs in his harms like a babby' (p. 95) – no mean feat for Dobbin to have accomplished with the drunken Jos. Again, in 'Sunday after the Battle', Becky is confronted with her swindling career by Trotter, the footman and the cook. 'Pay us our selleries' (p. 634), says the former, and poor Raggles asks 'Har you a goin' to pay me? You've lived in this 'ouse four year. You've 'ad my substances: my plate and linning. You ho me a milk and butter bill of two 'undred pound, you must 'ave noo-laid heggs for your homlets, and cream for your spanil dog' (p. 635). Here it is not merely the omitted aspirates, but the whole tone of the statement, which is so much in social as well as phonetic context.

The obviously satirical intent, as I have said, does not detract from the essential truth of utterance. James Crawley appears in one chapter; it is a tribute to Thackeray's range that he should be so convincing. Normally shy, he is released by drink into a forthright assertion of his own habits and culture. Nothing could be more damning in a University man. In effect, he puts his own pipe out:

'I'm none of your radicals. I know what it is to be a gentleman, dammy. See the chaps in a boat-race; look at the fellers in a fight; ay, look at a dawg killing rats – which is it wins? the good-blooded ones. Get some more port, Bowls, old boy, whilst I buzz this bottle here. What was I a saying?' (p. 407)

Accent and slang combine to make James truly his father's son, and a representative of a certain class; again the tone, here in inebriation, is caught to perfection.

Thackeray's parodic skill is also seen in his linguistic range. Thus in Brussels Isidor and Amelia's maid both utter French phrases evocative of despair and panic. In Isidor's case this is calculated to move Jos so that he can have the pick of Jos's wardrobe. Pauline is honest but frightened and in love – *'Tenez, Madame, est-ce qu'il n'est pas aussi à l'armée, mon homme à moi?'* (p. 359). This is the genuine idiom, but in Pumpernickel Jos with typical English grandeur assumes the language which, like Miss Pinkerton, he has never comprehended, with a *'Newmero kattervang dooze, si vous plait'* (p. 756), as he finds Becky's boarding-house room.

The spoken range in *Vanity Fair* is impressive, and the written perhaps even more so. We note the mannered writing of, for example, Miss Pinkerton, which is derived from the eighteenth century – so beloved by that lady who has received the patronage of the great lexicographer. The formal periods and the antithetical balance are evident in what we should correctly call her 'effusions':

Those virtues which characterise the young English gentlewoman, those accomplishments which become her birth and station, will not be found wanting in the amiable Miss Sedley, whose *industry* and *obedience* have endeared her to her instructors, and whose delightful sweetness of temper has charmed her *aged* and her *youthful* companions. (p. 40)

The italics are Miss Pinkerton's; the style is pompous, formal and artificial, like the woman. We see from the postscript to her letter to Mrs Bute that she can be vindictive too, saying of Becky, 'Though her appearance is disagreeable, we cannot control the operations of nature' (p. 135). She goes on to lie with a studied elegance and more italics.

As Kenneth Phillipps has noted, Miss Crawley and Miss Briggs also employ a kind of formal eighteenth-century idiom. Thackeray uses Richardson's epistolary manner cleverly by having Becky write her account of life at 'Humdrum Hall' in a manner very close to that of a Richardsonian heroine whipping up excitement before the next attempt on her virtue. It is of course parody, but since Becky is a parodist in her creator's manner, it is enjoyable too. Her letter in the chapter 'Arcadian Simplicity' closes in an unconsciously ironic manner:

Your Indian muslin and your pink silk, dearest Amelia, are said to become me very well. They are a good deal worn now; but, you know, we poor girls can't afford *des fraiches toilettes.* Happy, happy you! who have but to drive to St James's Street, and a dear mother who will give you anything you ask. (p. 139)

The irony is that Becky will always be adept at surviving poverty, while Amelia is to endure it in direct ratio to Becky's mounting success. The ironic letter is Thackeray's stylistic stock-in-trade but, as always, it offers layers of appreciation and we might note, in passing, Becky's use of the French phrase which is *her* stock-in-trade, being a Montmorency. Her letter to Rawdon after he has been arrested for debt has nine French phrases or words, a measure of her insincerity and affectation, her lack of grief and her *demi-mondaine* opportunism.

French words deliberately used because they reflect this fashionable affectation are often found in *Vanity Fair*, but Thackeray also uses them himself, sometimes without ironic intention, as when we read of the Belgian terrain that 'its wide *chaussées* swarmed with brilliant English equipages' (p. 325). Far more widespread in *Vanity Fair* is the use of jargon, sometimes French but more frequently English. We have seen James Crawley's slangy speech earlier, but such phrases as 'off the hooks' and 'to come up to scratch' are sometimes used in a tellingly ironic way, because of the context of supposed grandeur or nobility. Part of the naturalistic creation of character in *Vanity Fair* must be set down to the naturalness of speech. Sir Pitt is an '*old screw*', or so Becky reports in her letter to Amelia, 'which means a very stingy, avaricious person' (p. 110). Here we have the definition provided – Becky may be 'droll' but she is also accurate; she herself is described in commonplace racing slang as 'a neat little filly' (p. 138), which is the summit of imagination and beauty for Rawdon.

Georgy is puzzled by a glut of overheard slang when Major Loder – '"don't call *him* Major!" Emmy said' – tells Mrs Crawley 'No, no, Becky, you shan't keep the old buck to yourself. We must have the bones in, or dammy, I'll split' (p. 788). It has often been observed that Thackeray – the one-time Bohemian and gambler – is the master of the language of men about town who take their various forms: dandies, ne'er-do-wells, or what we would today call 'con' men like Rawdon. He also has the sporting jargon, so that a boxing match in which the result is faked, is referred to as a 'cross' (p. 639). Strong liquor is described as 'precious good tap', a watch is a 'ticker' and Dobbin is a 'spooney'. There are sometimes brilliantly ironic puns, as when Steyne considers that Becky is 'quite *killing*' in her charade role as Clytemnestra – a phrase which deliberately heralds what Thackeray calls her second appearance in that part, and the 'killing' of Jos.

From slang, often used with an ironic effect, it is but a short step to the consummate use of irony, which is employed at various levels throughout the novel. It is used kindly of Miss Jemima Pinkerton when, lacking her sister's superior accomplishments (though these do not include French), she speaks of a 'booky' for a 'bouquet' (p. 39). It is employed less kindly when Becky overdoes her language and emotion in the letter to Miss Briggs, informing her of her marriage to Rawdon – 'I leave the home where the poor orphan has ever met with kindness and affection' (p. 200). Irony is used with positive enjoyment in the description of Mr Veal, who undertakes the education of Georgy and uses many words where one would do. He describes Osborne senior's residence in Russell Square as 'your venerated grandfather's almost princely mansion', and as 'illuminated as if for the purposes of festivity. Am I right in my conjecture, that Mr Osborne entertained a society of chosen spirits round his sumptuous board last night?' (p. 655). Kenneth Phillipps has pointed out that Thackeray sometimes cleverly combines reported and direct speech, citing as an example George's late arrival for dinner, where a series of short sentences describe the rattling off of his excuses and conversation – an irritant to his father – in a kind of reported yet direct speech (p. 162). The effect is heavily ironic, since old Osborne has one thing in mind – the elimination of Amelia from George's life – while the reportage conveys the essentially superficial nature of George's mind, and his social irresponsibility.

The irony embraces Thackeray's fellow novelists. We remember the deletions from Chapter 6 ('Vauxhall'), but enough remains for us to see the author's delight in his small parodies of popular novelists. He ranges across the social scene from the aristocracy, to Mr Sedley's kitchen, to a professional burglar, before concluding with:

> But my readers must hope for no such romance, only a homely story, and must be content with a chapter about Vauxhall, which is so short that it scarce deserves to be called a chapter at all. And yet it is a chapter, and a very important one too. (p. 88)

This disclaimer is deliberately contrived, for the Vauxhall chapter is a microcosm of the world itself, and by analogy the world of *Vanity Fair*. This irony is further extended by the private joke with the reader; the chapter is *not* short, in fact it is somewhat longer than the two which precede and follow it – 'Dobbin of Ours', which has telling retrospect, and 'Crawley of Queen's Crawley' which, with a little history, gives us the immediate result of the Vauxhall visit. The irony lies in the manner and the tone, the attitude and the sleight of hand. 'Very important' is almost an understatement. Without Vauxhall, without the novelist providing the incident which changes lives naturally and not artificially, there would be no *Vanity Fair*; rack punch, like other accidents or indulgences, changes lives.

I have indicated earlier that Thackeray is the master of particular dialects, and these certainly constitute, in most instances, a form of irony. Becky's arrival at Great Gaunt Street has her putting the groom in his place for insolence. John's reply is noteworthy:

> 'I hope you've forgot nothink? Miss 'Melia's gownds – have you got them as the lady's-maid was to have 'ad. I hope they'll fit you. Shut the door, Jim, you'll get no good out of 'er ... a bad lot, I tell you, a bad lot.' (p. 104)

The effect of the irony here, as so often in *Vanity Fair*, is twofold. Becky is to become a progressively 'bad lot', while the downstairs greed is epitomized by John, whose eye for the main chance – the 'gownds' – is as sharp as Becky's. Moreover, Becky is now in the *real* world, and it is noticeable that the servant treats her for what she is – a scheming opportunist. Much, much later she is to be spoken to again like this, by servants she has swindled on a much greater scale, but this small example provides a foretaste of her future. Her gowns are never to be paid for.

The example above demonstrates the close connection between Thackeray's use of cockney dialect to convey a deeper intention, provoke a deeper reaction than mere laughter at words. Peggy O'Dowd's flow has been looked at on one level but there are others. There is a kindly, but at the same time structural irony in this:

> 'Fanny Magenis stops with her mother, who sells small coal and potatoes, most likely, in Islington-town, hard by London, though she's always bragging of her father's ships, and pointing them out to us as they go up the river; and Mrs Kirk and her children will stop here in Bethesda Place, to be nigh to her favourite preacher, Dr Ramshorn. Mrs Bunny's in an interesting situation – faith, and she always is, then ... And Ensign Posky's wife, who joined two months before you, my dear, has quarl'd with Tom Posky a score of times, till you can hear 'm all over the bar'ck (they say they're come to broken pleets, and Tom never accounted for his black oil.' (p. 320)

Now this is delightful, but there is much method in it. Firstly, there is the wide social reportage from the commercial, the religious, the 'interesting situation', to the rows. The irony plays in a kindly, indeed tolerant manner over Peggy's range, her gossipy, full-blown language covering the gamut of Vanity Fair. The irony is also forward-looking: Mr Sedley pathetically tries to sell coal later; the religious need, on another level, is to be provided by Lady Southdown; the 'interesting situation' is to be the blessing of Amelia's poor life and the bane of Becky's emergent one; while – and it would not be noticed if one didn't read carefully – Mrs Posky's incompatibility with Tom Posky is ultimately to lead to Glorvina securing a husband.

The humour again provides the surface, the skill a structural layer, in the ultimate working out of the novel in its broad definition of Vanity Fair. Selling, snobbery, religion, birth, love and quarrels are the stuff of *Vanity Fair*, here given a miniature focus. Peggy is not merely caricature; she carries much of the moral weight of the novel by her vivacious summary of its main concerns. And we notice, too, that there is just enough brogue to make her convincing, just enough of her other social register to make her real. Sometimes her truths are inescapable – 'It's not you are the only woman that are in the hands of God this day' (p. 368), she tells Amelia, and here the irony takes on a compassionate generality. The voice is Peggy's, the humanitarian truth the author's and, put into her mouth, the irony somehow acquires immediacy and perspective. Peggy's Vanity Fair is small compared with the one of profit and loss, glory and death.

The cockney and Irish dialects are not merely used as a humorous element. I think it is also true to say that Jos's Indian background is treated ironically, though the language is factual. 'Tiffin' (light meal, generally at noon), 'punkahs', 'tatties' (the latter are screens), Jos's own title of 'Collector' (the gathering in of revenues) and his magisterial presence at 'Cutcherry' (the court-house) all provided him with an authentic background. But the irony plays over his presentation, as we have seen in the section on his character. 'Waterloo Sedley', as he comes to be known, lives on his stories, and part of Thackeray's irony is to dwell upon these, for they mark the void in Jos's life – the constant repetition and indulgence of them being a substitute for living. There is also, linked to this, a Thackerayan irony on a broader scale, which conveys that too much living in the past is wrong. Jos's stories, on a lightly ironic level, are equivalent to Amelia's dwelling on the only 'past' she knows – those brief (despoiled) honeymoon days with George.

Worship of the past, says the author ironically, is chaos in the present, and this applies in its different ways to the whole Sedley family. Dobbin, of course, also dwells too much in the past, but here the irony is a pathetic index to time wasted – something that he becomes aware of, as he at last honestly acknowledges how Amelia has undervalued his love. The sublime moment of irony in the novel which shows the indelible connection of past and present is Becky's. Her revelation of how that 'low-bred cockney dandy, that padded booby, who had neither wit, nor manners, nor heart' (p. 789) had offered to elope with her on the eve of Waterloo is the bluntest and most ironic castigation in the whole of the novel. Although dead, George has been living in Amelia's memory, but Becky's words kill him off forever. The irony again operates on another level as well as this obvious one: the revelation comes too late. Although the forms are gone through and Dobbin marries Amelia, we are left in no doubt that the Colonel (and Amelia) will live with his consciousness of waste and error. It would be impossible here to indicate the range of Thackerayan irony, either in the stylistic or thematic sense, for it runs throughout *Vanity Fair* and is indeed the substance of the novel.

Areas of parody have already been given, and parody partakes of irony. We might consider in passing the use of proper names (Crawley, Eaves, Steyne, Pitt, Bute), but if we did so we should have to look not merely at sound but at historical/moral associations as well. As Kenneth Phillipps observes, Thackeray 'clearly enjoyed exercising his wit in such *tours de force* of nomenclature'. Superb examples are to be found in the tracing of the Crawley lineage (pp. 101–2), and the 'melancholy end of that nobleman', Lord Steyne (p. 753). But there is often an ironic counterbalance to the fictional elevation which provides the moral reality. Thus the description of the Crawleys is followed by Sir Pitt's letter to Becky:

> Sir Pitt Crawley begs Miss Sharp and baggidge may be here on Tuesday, as I leaf for Queen's Crawley to-morrow morning *erly*. (p. 102)

Notice that Thackeray does not overdo the misspelling; there is just enough to indicate the difference between what appears to be a distinguished family, and what is the common reality of lack of culture.

The same technique is used after the catalogue of Steyne's positions, where we have the sycophantic praise of the degraded nobleman followed by the sordid attempts of Madame de Belladonna to retain 'the banknotes, jewels, Neapolitan and French bonds, etc., found in his Lordship's secretaire, and claimed by his heirs from that injured woman' (p. 754). I suppose that 'Belladonna' is one of the more obvious of Thackeray's ironic names, though perhaps Dobbin's is even more so in a 'Novel without a Hero'.

The most brilliant use of names, however, is left to the very end and, as the Tillotsons have pointed out, the choice of 'Burke, Thurtell & Hayes' (p. 796) is a subtle underlining of Becky's motives in securing Jos. They are the names of her solicitors who defend her right to the legacy from Jos; they are also the names of three convicted murderers. This ironic element cannot be ignored. Both Dickens and Thackeray used names with great deliberation and intent to set up associations (witness Mr Merdle in *Little Dorrit*, from French *merde* – excrement), but Thackeray, because of his historical *and* journalistic verve, is able to provide a subtext, often moral in implication, to his own novel. The result is a further enrichment of the reader's experience and enjoyment.

Thackeray's parody embraces a number of areas. For example, in Chapter 4 he has Becky sing a song (one of his own verses) which has a certain pathetic quality. It is a parody of many such songs, but the appropriateness of Becky's singing something sentimental and false (afterwards 'her deep-toned voice faltered' – yet another contemporary reference) is attended by a social placing. By this I mean that it is a drawing-room song, well distanced from the experience it describes. The moral-ironic emphasis is apparent, as in Thackeray's descriptions of the ruining of small tradesmen in the wake of society swindlers like Becky. Yet another parody carries with it an implicit comment, a judgement important in *Vanity Fair* and approximating in some ways to Dickens's indictment of Mrs Pardiggle and Mrs Jellyby in *Bleak House*. If Lady Southdown is 'Lady Macbeth' in terms of tracts and medicines, then Lady Emily is in the great tradition of daughters who follow in their mothers' footsteps, and unfortunately those footsteps lead towards print. What Thackeray describes as 'that beautiful poem' is a parody from his own hand:

> 'Lead us to some sunny isle,
> Yonder in the western deep;
> Where the skies for ever smile,
> And the blacks for ever weep,' etc. (p. 392)

This is more than tongue in cheek: the insipid quality of the verse, with its easy antithesis and naïve form, reflects the easy assumption of piety which is distanced from experience. This perspective is finely sustained in the tract titles – the 'Washerwoman of Finchley Common' and 'Fleshpots Broken: or, the Converted Cannibal' (p. 395). Writing about life or religion is the substitute for actually living; and we even learn that the long-suffering and deprived spinster Miss Briggs is the authoress of 'Lyrics of the Heart', a title entirely appropriate to one who has never had any such experiences because of her selfless devotion to Miss Crawley and, later, to little Rawdon.

Allied to parody and the insistent irony is satire, and here Thackeray explores particular areas of society and behaviour with the probing touch of the moralist. In a sense, *Vanity Fair* is a satire throughout, but it is underpinned by kindliness, tolerance, humanity and compassion for the follies of ambition and social advancement which are exposed. The visit to Pumpernickel (Weimar) gives Thackeray the opportunity to indulge his reminiscences in a satirical vein, whether it be at the expense of the ostentatious Court, the political quarrels or the hierarchical grouping. One character receives the full treatment:

> Lord Tapeworm inherited no little portion of the family gallantry, and it was his happy belief, that almost every woman upon whom he himself cast friendly eyes, was in love with him. He left Emmy under the persuasion that she was slain by his wit and attractions, and went home to his lodgings to write a pretty little note to her. (p. 726)

In these words Thackeray exposes the vanity of his title, pillories the egoist, scorns the pompous and inflated position of his character and holds up to the bewildered Emmy the mirror of her departed George, in which she still cannot see the reflection. It is an entirely suitable choice of person – and of place – for Emmy's real education to begin. Against the background of culture (which is good for her, since she has been deprived of it) and of superficial behaviour, she has ultimately to face up to the reality of Dobbin's love for her, and her own wish to retain him. The Pumpernickel episode, with its studied satirical tone and its exposure of what Barbara Hardy has called 'luxury', is climactic to the novel. Once more the focus is microcosmic. Pumpernickel equals the much larger world, its characters as fake and opportunist as the characters of London and Hampshire.

I want now to look at another aspect of Thackeray's style, and that is the consummate way in which he builds up to a climax. This is linked to the foregoing paragraph, in the sense that it describes society at play and follows it with a terrible reality. The chapters here referred to are 51, 52 and 53 – the acting of the charades and the release of Rawdon through Lady Jane, followed by his discovery of Steyne and Becky together. Kenneth Phillipps has said of Chapter 51 that 'The whole chapter is a tone poem, ending on this note of quiet ominousness [the arrest of Rawdon], presaging the stormy climax of the novel.' There is something in this, but much more is attributable to the cunning satire involved in the actual choice of charades – the display which conceals the reality to come and deludes us (and Rawdon, though he has glimmers) into a sense of false security. Firstly, there is the exoticism of the first charade, in which Mrs Winkworth takes the centre stage and is afterwards complimented by Becky. The switch to the Grecian scene has Rawdon as 'The King of men' (p. 595) and Becky as Clytemnestra. The interaction prompts Steyne's 'Brava, brava', as Becky acts her part to perfection. She and Mrs Winkworth as Zuleikah take the applause, but in the next charade Becky eclipses everybody by being 'the NIGHTINGALE of the evening' (p. 599). There follows an account of Becky's rising triumph as everyone who is anyone seeks her company; perhaps the most important statement of all being that 'Lord Steyne was her slave' (p. 600).

I suggest that a close look at these charades reveals both a satirical intention and a consummate sense of structure. Mrs Winkworth is eclipsed by Becky as Amelia was in life; Rawdon is a king of men in the moral sense, and proves to be so in the next chapter. He knocks down Steyne, overturning with one blow the false acting of his wife and her paramour – of which these charades are a parody. Thackeray's own climactic sense and satirical verve have Becky acclaimed for what she is, in intention if not in practice: a 'nightingale', contemporary slang for a prostitute, in the highest and perhaps most corrupt level of society.

Again the interplay between the outside world and this world of acting is made obvious by the choice of scene, even by the innocent song ('The Rose upon my Balcony'), for all is corruption, display and thrusting ambition as distinct from reality. The perfect climax to the chapter is presented almost as anti-climax, just as life is anti-climactic after some escapist experience – a 'charade' seen on the television, for example. By choosing this select interior, Thackeray is once more emphasizing the differences between illusion and reality. Rawdon's arrest is real and changes his life – and Becky's. Becky's triumphs – like the charades – are illusory, and she will be exposed to other kinds of reality. The balance within the chapter is superbly controlled. New readers of the novel can hardly anticipate the arrest of Rawdon, metaphorically stabbed in the back by the Clytemnestra he has subjugated himself to.

Chapter 52, as if the crescendo is unfinished, extends the realism at the expense of the delusion (a better word than illusion in this context). The irony gives way to a leisured retrospect on Lord Steyne's machinations – the removal of little Rawdon to school, the arrangement of another situation for Briggs – before returning us, in Chapter 53, to Rawdon, his pathetic letter, Becky's affected reply, the dramatic release of Rawdon by Lady Jane and his return to Curzon Street. In this chapter we see Thackeray's style at its economical best – graphic, immediate and dramatic in action and dialogue. In under two pages the scene and its aftermath are reported without a word wasted. Becky's 'I am innocent' (p 620) at the beginning is repeated vainly at the end. Thackeray always gives the impression of having time for leisurely narration, of spreading out the content of his scenes and incidents. Here he shows that the impression is sometimes false, and this scene is as tensely climactic as the paragraph which reports the death of George Osborne at the end of Chapter 32.

No mention has yet been made in this commentary of Thackeray's use of imagery: it is true to say that allusion and historical/contemporary reference bulk larger in *Vanity Fair*. But of the many scattered images throughout *Vanity Fair*, two, both moral in import, stand out and I intend to focus on these. In the scene just referred to, we are told of Becky that:

> The wretched woman was in a brilliant full toilette, her arms and all her fingers sparkling with bracelets and rings ... She clung hold of his coat, of his hands; her own were all covered with serpents, and rings, and baubles.

Her second 'I am innocent' follows this, but we should note not only the jewellery, symbolic itself of one of the great vanities of Vanity Fair, but particularly the connection of serpents with innocence.

Becky is the temptress, the analogy is with the Garden of Eden, for serpent/reptilian imagery is a moral index in the novel. A fine anticipation of this occurs in Chapter 44, and it will indicate the overall awareness and structure of the novel. In that chapter, Becky boxes little Rawdon's ears for listening to her singing (and of course for being in her way with Lord Steyne); we learn that she is 'writhing' towards 'a position in society' (p. 523). Linked to this is another anticipation which reverses Becky's own declaration of innocence in Chapter 53. Two paragraphs earlier Thackeray has written, ' "Was Rebecca guilty or not?" The Vehmgericht [secret court] of the servants' hall had pronounced against her' (p. 523). He had earlier referred to 'the awful kitchen inquisition which sits in judgment in every house, and knows everything' (p. 522). The imagery is linked to a consummate ironic perspective; the servants know before Rawdon does. It is the upstairs-downstairs interaction given a studied moral emphasis.

There is another sequence – here a mermaid-cum-fish image, which is obviously connected with the serpent imagery quoted above. The opening of the final double number has an authorial lightness of touch, already referred to in a previous section, which conveys through its images the nature of Becky's promiscuity, while observing the limits of convention by this cunning disclaimer:

> In describing this siren, singing and smiling, coaxing and cajoling ... has he once forgotten the laws of politeness, and showed the monster's hideous tail above water? No! Those who like may peep down under waves that are pretty transparent, and see it writhing and twirling, diabolically hideous and slimy, flapping amongst bones, or curling round corpses ... (p. 738)

This is not all; for Thackeray goes on to refer to the siren as being among the dead men, describing the waters as growing 'turbid over her', and then considers the innocence projected by the mermaid sitting on the rock with her looking-glass. All this adds up to a moral condemnation of Becky and her kind through a deliberate use of the imagery of temptation, which leads to the death of the tempted. There is little doubt that the analogy is sexual, but it is moral as well, with Becky's 'killing' of Rawdon (and possibly Jos in the future) and her luring others to destruction, like the servants. Lord Steyne, epitomizing evil, only just escapes the 'mermaid'; and Becky herself sinks into the slimy waters of a degraded existence before she surfaces again into respectability. Sexual reticence is integral to Victorian fiction; Thackeray, through the use of reptilian and fish imagery, goes some way towards explicitness.

Perhaps the most quoted image in *Vanity Fair* is that used by Thackeray himself in an ironic description of the Amelia–Dobbin marriage. A succession of images precede it – 'vessel', 'prize', 'port', 'bird', 'billing and cooing', 'outstretched wings' – a kind of pathetic panorama of clichéd reference, in order to convey the anti-climax, the loss inherent in that final coming together. It is rounded off with, 'Grow green again, tender little parasite, round the rugged old oak to which you cling!' (p. 792). In a perceptive note, John Sutherland has pointed out the derivations of this – Horace and *Paradise Lost*, with a later echo in *Henry Esmond* – as well as indicating the full effect of the image, which is certainly 'the ironic contradiction of fertile union and strangulating clingingness'. This is right, but it goes beyond that: for it is a brilliant reversal of what has gone before, and at the same time a deliberate identification with it. Dobbin has *clung* 'for fifteen years in vain' (p. 776), and Amelia has *clung* with parasitic intensity to the memory of George. The implication is that the growth which reaches back will continue into the future; present and past are given an emotional continuum.

There is no change; the rooted tendencies (I choose the words deliberately) will spread, but they will become more diseased with the passing of time. The habit of nature becomes the habit of human nature – there is no accompanying elevation. Amelia needs Dobbin, and Dobbin cannot escape from the emotional ivy which has clung round him for fifteen years. The choice of qualifying words is important too, and shows how carefully Thackeray adapted the popular conception to fit his characters. Amelia is 'tender' and Dobbin is 'rugged'; the first conveys not only her capacity for love, but also its overweening nature. The second conveys the ability to withstand anything, but also the obduracy needed to do so. A common image is therefore given an incisive individuality. The rugged man will love his daughter and write his 'History of the Punjaub'; the tender little woman will have her every whim gratified. Behind her the shadow of Mrs Brookfield bulks large; the effect is one of muted mutuality, of accepted bondage rather than shared delight. It is the final comment on two of the characters with whom we have lived, but whose lives are conditioned by the past.

Much has been made, and rightly, of what John Sutherland calls 'The Iphigenia Scene' in *Vanity Fair* (see *Thackeray at Work*, pp. 11–17). Here I intend to demonstrate its symbolic force within the novel. The 'chronometer, which was surrounded by a cheerful brass group of the sacrifice of Iphigenia' (p. 161), is mentioned in Chapter 13, which has the appropriately ironic title, 'Sentimental and Otherwise' – the last word embracing Mr Osborne's plans to prevent George from marrying a bankrupt's daughter. Iphigenia was the daughter of Agamemnon and Clytemnestra (the connection with Becky will be obvious), who was sacrificed at Aulis (according to Aeschylus), though perhaps escaped (according to Euripides). Dobbin's visit to Miss Osborne in propitiation for George's marriage to Amelia begins with silence, a symbolic counterpart as the measure of time, and of sacrifice – 'the tick-tock of the Sacrifice of Iphigenia clock on the mantelpiece became quite rudely audible' (p. 268). As Jane Osborne much later waits on and housekeeps for her lonely father – her own loneliness is much the greater of the two – she works at her piece of worsted by the fire 'hard by the great Iphigenia clock, which ticked and tolled with mournful loudness in the dreary room' (p. 502).

The clock is the symbol of sacrifice, but it is also the symbol of lack of taste, of the vulgarity which Mrs Maria Bullock, now moving in a different circle, comes to despise in her father. But to merely equate the symbolism with Becky and Amelia is to be simplistic: it must be equated with the sacrifice of George by his father (and, symbolically, with the sacrifices that father has made in the past for his conceited and snobbish son). Since it measures time, the clock must also be equated with Amelia's sacrifice of her son (a nicely ironic touch indeed, that little George should return to the sphere where that clock is), Amelia's virtual sacrifice of her mother in favour of her son (a reversal of the Clytemnestra/Iphigenia position) and the many other sacrifices in the novel. Nor is this all. If Iphigenia did escape, then it gives an added relevance to Amelia coming into money and going to Pumpernickel, forced to sacrifice her memory of George for the reality of Dobbin (in one of the Iphigenia stories, she makes sacrifices at the command of the goddess). Here Clytemnestra reverses her role: it is Becky who sacrifices that sordid little incident with George, by telling Amelia of George's past infatuation for her.

Sutherland demonstrates that the manuscript of *Vanity Fair* contains an alteration which makes this Iphigenia sequence even more weighted with authorial irony. Thackeray originally wrote Jephthah (who had to sacrifice his child in the Bible), and then crossed it out in favour of Iphigenia. The pagan replaces the biblical, thus according with old Osborne's materialistic sacrifice of his son. The word 'cheerful' in the first Iphigenia reference is not crossed out, and appears to be directly ironic; yet strangely there is even some doubt here. In some versions of the story, Iphigenia's 'sacrifice' is halted before the descent of the executioner's axe. This would explain the word 'cheerful', though the clock is obviously a representation from Racine's tragedy, *Iphigénie* (1674). Significantly, in the privacy of old Osborne's study, without the ostentatious display of clock, plate and furniture, Thackeray reverts to the Bible to compare the old man's inner state with his outward irascibility. He takes down the great red Bible, 'seldom looked at, and shining all over with gold' (p. 281). The frontispiece represents Abraham sacrificing his son, Isaac, and Osborne proceeds to sacrifice his son in the name of the Lord of Ambition, Status and Money – the unholy trinity of Vanity Fair. This shows Thackeray's use of particular symbols to comment on his own moral concerns in *Vanity Fair*.

Thackeray is also adept at the mock-heroic vein. Early in the novel (Chapter 4), he elevates the Cuff–Dobbin fight by employing just such a manner to describe the end of that contest:

If I had the pen of a Napier, or a Bell's Life, I should like to describe this combat properly. It was the last charge of the Guard – (that is, it *would* have been, only Waterloo had not yet taken place) – it was Ney's column breasting the hill of La Haye Sainte, bristling with ten thousand bayonets, and crowned with twenty eagles – it was the shout of the beef-eating British, as leaping down the hill they rushed to hug the enemy in the savage arms of battle – in other words, Cuff coming up full of pluck, but quite reeling and groggy, the Fig-merchant put in his left as usual on his adversary's nose, and sent him down for the last time. (p. 82)

The humour at the expense of serious history and sporting reportage is qualified once again by a sense of relevance and anticipation – Waterloo has not yet happened, but is going to be the crucial centrepiece of the novel's action. It will change lives, just as this small encounter changes lives, giving Dobbin the respect and friendship of George, his own focal point for as long as George lives and afterwards devotion to his widow. If the introduction of Dobbin was something of an afterthought, there is no doubting his integration into the main action of the novel.

I have tried in this section to indicate the main facets of Thackeray's style in *Vanity Fair*. I have also tried, by association and implication, to show that Thackeray's style subsumes a wider area of the novel, and that is its structure. In the sections on 'The Teller in his Tale', 'Characterization' and that dealing with 'Plot and Action', I have indicated that Thackeray, despite improvisations, was constantly aware of his structure. Indeed everything is related to everything else, and nothing in *Vanity Fair* is extraneous to the exposition and exposure of society. Thackeray was not a casual writer, despite the rigour of serial publication, with its attendant anecdotes of how he wrote with the postboy waiting at the door for the printer's copy.

There is evidence, as we move backwards and forwards in the text, of meticulous planning, of forecasting situations and of verbal associations, which are set up so that they may be echoed later. The aesthetic balance, the great sweep embracing the accretion of cumulative detail, is not merely artistically pleasing; it has its moral correlative as well. Thus Amelia's great experiences in life are set on the continent, away from the main sweep of Vanity Fair – the first, her loss of George (and her unvoiced knowledge of his, at least, moral infidelity), the second, her eventual discovery of Dobbin's worth and her own self-discovery. In parallel to this, one may say that Becky rises and falls on the continent (post-Waterloo) as well as in London (post-Steyne); and that she and Amelia have, in different ways, a social position – Amelia's in Hampshire, Becky's a somewhat shadowy respectability in Cheltenham.

The pattern of parallel and contrast is maintained throughout the novel, and if its outline is simplistic, the effects are striking. Sedley falls, Osborne rises; arguably, adversity is not more sour than the miserable isolation of success. Little George and little Rawdon have rather different upbringings; arguably, little Rawdon turns out somewhat the better, his surrogate mother, with her gentle but unobtrusive kindliness, proving more effective in influence than Amelia. Behind both children is their heredity: Rawdon's inherent goodness outweighs his wife's unscrupulous rejection of the child, while George's vanity and conceit outweigh Amelia's tenderness in little George. I could go on citing parallels indefinitely. The fact is, they exist and complement each other on all levels of *Vanity Fair*. It would be too simple to say the style *is* the structure, though it would in part be true. It is perhaps better to say that within the multiple styles of *Vanity Fair*, one finds the essential multiplicity of the novel drawn into a coherent and expansive form. Art and artifice construct the fictional artefact, consciously and consummately, and the result is an emotional, intellectual and aesthetic experience, redolent of wisdom and, above all, of the nature of life.

Conclusion

Vanity Fair and some Nineteenth-century Novels

The title of *Vanity Fair* is taken from Section 4 of *The Pilgrim's Progress* (1678) by John Bunyan (1628–88), and, as we know, the idea for that title came to Thackeray quite suddenly. Christian and Faithful, on their continuing journey, arrive in Vanity Fair, where they are tried because of the impression they have created. Faithful is condemned to be burnt and tortured, but Christian is allowed to proceed. There is no straightforward analogy, on a character-by-character level, between Bunyan's narrative and Thackeray's, but there is an analogy in terms of moral purpose. The tone is completely different, but just as Bunyan's allegory deals with a journey through life, so does Thackeray's – though on a rather broader level. Just as there are a series of obstacles and temptations in *The Pilgrim's Progress*, so there are in *Vanity Fair*.

But whereas Thackeray's novel is rooted in social and historical reality, Bunyan's is rooted in a different kind of reality – the reality of the vision or dream. The temptations of Bunyan's vision are abstractions made visually concrete; the temptations of *Vanity Fair* are real in their social and moral context. Christian survives through spiritual faith; Dobbin, for example, through individual integrity. There are other parallels and points of correspondence between the two books, but the two authors themselves are so far apart in time, faith and background, that it would be pointless to extend this investigation. My aim here is to indicate the greatness of *Vanity Fair* by setting it in its literary context, to compare Thackeray with his great contemporaries and one of his great successors, George Eliot, particularly in *Middlemarch*.

As *Vanity Fair* was being published, *Dombey and Son* was also being issued in monthly numbers. On reading of the death of little Paul, Thackeray was moved to say that there was 'no writing against' that, though he had felt that he was now at the top of the literary tree fighting it out with Dickens. By the time he published *Dombey and Son*, Dickens was unquestionably the greatest of Thackeray's contemporaries. It is my contention that in *Dombey and Son*, Dickens shows for the first time a mature sense of *form*, a feeling for the inter-relatedness of all segments of his novel as being part of its artistic whole. Yet *Dombey and Son* seems to me to possess weaknesses which are not present in *Vanity Fair*, although there are many points of connection with Thackeray's novel. Walter Gay, Captain Cuttle and Solomon Gills exist on a different level of caricature than anything in *Vanity Fair*, but Dickens's social range is greater than Thackeray's, and there is a vivacity which compensates for the excess of sentiment.

Like Thackeray, Dickens is concerned with the large world of finance and business; but whereas Thackeray deals with the West End, Dickens deals with the City and related areas. Dickens is concerned with obsession, as in Mr Dombey, and this is his great strength; Thackeray is concerned with the panorama of individual relationships set against the tide of history, and this is his. Interestingly, both take their characters away from the main centre of the action – Thackeray to the continent (and to Brighton), Dickens to Leamington, to the continent (Carker's flight and Mr Dombey's pursuit) and also to Brighton (Dr Blimber's academy for Paul). I think it would be pointless to draw further comparisons.

Dombey and Son is a great novel, full of vivacity, imagination, graphic description, social and moral concern, brilliant visual creations, humour, pathos and all that characterizes 'the inimitable' in Dickens's works. His voice, like Thackeray's, is informed with wisdom and compassion. If we set the two books beside each other we become aware of remarkable differences, and yet note that they are recognizably of the same period. Dickens is concerned with the inherent evils in society, and so is Thackeray. Each is a strongly moral writer, Thackeray making his points through irony and satire, Dickens through the exposure and indictment of poor conditions.

Both are realists in different ways, not in the full expression of psychologically developed characters, but in the distinct appraisal of recognizable character traits – from pride to egoism, goodness to self-indulgence, kindness to jealousy and from hate to love. Yet it seems to me that Thackeray, in *Vanity Fair*, is a much more ambivalent writer. As he presents us with Florence Dombey, or with Paul, no doubt exists in Dickens's mind of their intrinsic virtue. But Thackeray, as we have seen, was fully aware of Amelia's culpability, not only in her attitude towards Dobbin, but also in her overweening protection of little George and her obsessional blindness with regard to her husband. For Dickens goodness is often unsullied; for Thackeray it is usually qualified. The same applies to their respective treatments of evil. There are no redeeming features in Carker, but even in old Osborne and, in passing, in Becky (as when she ensures that Amelia will have Dobbin), there is that movement of human nature which occurs in life against the predominant traits of character.

But Dickens's greatest works are *Bleak House* (1852–3) and *Little Dorrit* (1855–7), and in both the satirical attack mounted on society has many parallels with that of Thackeray, though the key emphasis is different. In *Bleak House* the fog of the Law is the main focus, and the ramifications, the tentacular results, together with the complicated revelations of the plot involving Lady Dedlock, make it a great but uneven novel. The satire on missionary work is superbly sustained, as Dickens exposes the social evils under the noses of people like Mrs Jellyby, who brings everything to bear on zealous conversion on the banks of the Niger, at the expense of her own family and the immediate concerns about her. The brickmaker's family, the sufferings of Caddy and her father, the superb Regency Mr Turveydrop and the parasitic Skimpole, are beyond Thackeray's social range. But *Bleak House* has one serious narrative flaw, and critics intent on examining the fineness of its structure, and the social compassion evident in the presentation of Jo, tend to explain or even overlook the narrative failure, which divides the novel between the narrative voice of Charles Dickens on the one hand, and the supposed narration of Esther Summerson on the other. The effect is somewhat cloying, with Esther a symbol of goodness before her illness, and her tone and her love for Woodcourt both far from convincing.

There are no comparable errors of balance or tone in Thackeray; the narrator has a firm grasp of his material, and *his* narration and overview are consistent. If we turn to *Little Dorrit* we find a great advance in structural coherence. Again the satire is the mainspring, with the Circumlocution Office approximating to the Law in *Bleak House*. But the Marshalsea prison, and the prison imagery of society outside, – witness the high financier and swindler, Mr Merdle, and his almost reticent suicide – show Dickens closer to Thackeray here than elsewhere. The social and society areas are different, the Blandois–Flintwich plot totally alien to the way Thackeray worked, but glorious comic creations like Flora Finching and Mr F.'s aunt show Dickens's own range, a range which embraces The Bosom and Bar, as well as a host of Barnacles and the superb William Dorrit – as fine a psychological portrait as one may find anywhere in Dickens.

Journeys, like the journeys in *Vanity Fair*, are important. In a curious way Mr Dorrit's position and collapse in Rome have structural connections with the society of Brussels, which Thackeray so brilliantly presents. As Little Dorrit feels, 'this same society in which they lived, greatly resembled a superior sort of Marshalsea' (Book II, Chapter 7), and this is the kind of notation which makes for a unifying adhesive in *Vanity Fair*. Mr Moss's establishment in Cursitor Street, to which Rawdon is taken – and where he is very well known and received – mirrors the outside world of Vanity Fair, just as the Marshalsea does, and there are many points of contact between these two great novels.

On another level, *Little Dorrit* is also a novel without a hero, for Clennam is as unlikely as Dobbin to fill that role. Yet both Dickens and Thackeray are fundamentally right in their presentations of such a character, for both are close to life – Dobbin, despite his cartoon name and appearance, and Clennam, despite his age and a certain world-weariness. The difference is that whereas Dobbin develops from a gangling and clumsy youth of dubious social credentials, into an efficient, well-loved officer, Clennam develops but little, even as the revelations of his own life emerge. This is not to say that Clennam is a failure; far from it. He is a finely realized character, his realism all the more remarkable in view of his reticence.

Again we are made aware of the correspondences and differences of two great novelists exposing the nature of humanity and society. And it must be said that both present us with an essential truth. Thackeray, for all the accusations of cynicism, is perhaps the more optimistic – or perhaps realistic – of the two. Dickens kills off or punishes his morally culpable characters; Thackeray kills off Steyne, but Becky lives on with her acquired respectability. Dickens's social and moral indignation permeates his fiction; Thackeray's irony, tolerance and humanitarian wisdom permeate his.

If we move on twenty-four years to George Eliot's *Middlemarch* (1871–2), we notice a great advance in imaginative, technical and, above all, psychological achievement. Its subtitle, 'A Study of Provincial Life', sufficiently defines its area. But like the prison of Dickens, the London and Brussels of Thackeray, Middlemarch is the mirror of larger, greater and universal societies. The essential difference is that George Eliot, certainly as fine a moralist and compassionate ironist as Thackeray, focuses on human relationships from within. To take a simple comparison, the Dorothea–Casaubon marriage, like the Lydgate–Rosamond one, is viewed through the stormy interaction of the individual with the partner who shares his or her lot. Casaubon's austere and frigid proposal to Dorothea is consistent with his subsequent behaviour; but the motives, which are the mainspring of behaviour, are exposed through to the nerve-ends.

Jealously possessive of his arid learning and frightened that its archaic nature will be exposed by the young wife, who has misguidedly accepted him, thinking she could be a helpmeet, Casaubon moves slowly from unhappiness and insecurity to death – and even after death the contents of his will rule his widow. Lydgate succumbs to a pair of forget-me-not blue eyes in a moment of weakness, and finds himself ruled by an inflexible will which ultimately destroys his medical idealism and practicality. As Lydgate puts it, Rosamond becomes his basil-plant. Highly sophisticated and appropriate imagery accompanies the narration of individual anguish, or individual indulgence – images of the web, the window, the tomb, for example – thus giving the novel a texture which is both human and intellectual. Like *Vanity Fair*, *Middlemarch* is set in the past, its action covering the era 1829–32 – the period of the first great Reform Bill.

Complementing the political reform ethos is a stress on the emergence of medical reform, the coming of the railways, the traditional social hierarchy of a provincial town and, more important than all else, the dilemmas and decisions which face individuals. For George Eliot's major concern is always with the individual conscience, and though her own voice is used omnisciently, it is not as frequently employed in commentary or evaluation as Thackeray's. The idealism of Lydgate is snuffed out (the aspiring reformer writes a treatise on gout – the rich man's disease), while Dorothea's idealism is muted rather than erased. Her infinite capacity for good does not centre in 'some long-recognizable deed', but is devoted to the everyday welfare of others by example and practice.

The conclusion, or more correctly the Finale – equivalent to the last part of the last chapter in *Vanity Fair* – is optimistic but realistic, for George Eliot's moral philosophy does not shrink from the truth of life as it is. There is in *Middlemarch* a timelessness which transcends period, and it is great because of that. There is a similar timelessness about *Vanity Fair*, as I have indicated in this commentary. The intellectualism of George Eliot, like that of Henry James, moves the novel into the category of high art. Frederic Harrison, reading George Eliot's previous novel, *Felix Holt*, observed that one needed to give every phrase the close attention which one would normally give to poetry such as *In Memoriam*, since the range and depth of association – in poetry compressed, in the novel expansive – merited such discipline. I would suggest that *Vanity Fair* should be accorded the same disciplined reading, and indeed the editions and novels cited in the Further Reading section which follows, indicate the close attention accorded to it by scholars and critics.

Vanity Fair is a unique novel. Nowhere else, except perhaps in Shakespeare and Tolstoy, do we feel the effect of breadth and depth at the same time. I have drawn comparisons here with a great contemporary of Thackeray's, and a great successor. But if we looked at the other significant novels published during 1847–8, we should find that *Vanity Fair* dwarfs them, not merely in bulk but in stature. Mrs Tillotson, in *Novels of the Eighteen-Forties* (1954), has already drawn attention to the particular merits of *Dombey and Son*, Mrs Gaskell's *Mary Barton* (1848) and Charlotte Brontë's *Jane Eyre* (1847). Mrs Tillotson says it all when she observes of the first that 'though a distinguished novel, [it] is hardly of the scale or the quality of the other three novels here selected' (one of which was *Vanity Fair*). Of *Mary Barton* she says that it is 'primarily a novel of the inner life, not of man in his social relations; it maps a private world'. This is true, and it defines the difference in range precisely. *Jane*

Eyre is subtitled 'An Autobiography', and this is a sufficiently teasing attraction; but it is an autobiography in the imaginative rather than the authentic sense – wish-fulfilment, and independent decision – a remarkable achievement from a literary backwater. Its time and place are virtually irrelevant, though we may identify Cowan Bridge School and ponder on the life and practices of the Rev. Carus Wilson.

Charlotte Brontë recognized (somewhat to Thackeray's embarrassment) the nature of his achievement. But the whole force of her background and that of her inner personality could create great fiction – though there are periods of aridity and over-writing in *Jane Eyre* – without any of the Thackerayan ambivalence. *Jane Eyre* and *Vanity Fair* share a publication date, but little else. The compulsive lure of *Jane Eyre* is allied to emotional identification on the part of the reader; the lure of *Vanity Fair* is the contemplation of the motives and actions of the fictional and historically placed characters – symbols of ourselves for all time. *Vanity Fair* sees into the human heart and exposes it without bitterness; *Jane Eyre* penetrates the individual imagination and exposes it with dramatic verve. Strangely, there is some analogy with *The Pilgrim's Progress* in *Jane Eyre*; Jane's journeys lead to encounters, temptations and decisions. *Jane Eyre* is a strongly individual work, but although carefully structured, it is uneven; the Gothic elements – the melodramatic incidents, the pattern of coincidence and the mystical happy ending – are set uneasily beside the compulsive realism of the early chapters.

Mary Barton has been underrated until recently, but it cannot be placed beside *Vanity Fair*. Mrs Gaskell's strength is in her social realism, her weakness is melodrama and the conscious imposition of the theme of reconciliation. She is a fine novelist in *North and South*, where the psychology of character, the social interaction as well as the emotional, is superbly delineated. Also, in the late-flowering *Wives and Daughters*, her irony, the delicacy and yet incisiveness of her perception, are seen at their best.

But one other novel must be taken into account, if only because it was published in the same year as *Vanity Fair*, and has since achieved a greater popularity. I refer of course to *Wuthering Heights*, Emily Brontë's novel, which is unique in English fiction. I say unique because it seems to me to be a book which goes beyond morality, beyond its time, and yet has an artistic structure and integrity which set it apart from literary and living conventions. It is a work rich in the individual imagination, its setting and modes of narration – primarily through Lockwood and Nelly Dean – establish dramatic immediacy with the reader. But whereas in *Vanity Fair* we are always aware of the narrator, in *Wuthering Heights* we are aware of the narrator *in* her creations. Emily Brontë does not need her own voice, because *Wuthering Heights is* her own voice in the multiple experiences of her characters.

The moors are felt as strongly as Egdon Heath in *The Return of the Native* (1878), but there is no moral gloss, no sense of fate and no wide social perspective. Yet such is Emily's sophistication – I use the word deliberately to emphasize the careful artistic structure – that the chronology is meticulous. That chronology – which spans the years 1771 to 1802 – is of a piece with the rest of the novel. *Wuthering Heights* is a world of its own: the perspective is finely sustained. It is almost too simple to say that revenge and violence, like ultimate harmony, are themes in a novel which goes beyond theme and character, and exists not, as F. R. Leavis once wrote, as a 'kind of sport', but as a poem and a reality simultaneously. The subtlety with which the narratives are interwoven (consider Isabella's letter about her life with Heathcliff) is further exemplified in the exposure of relationships, passionate intensity and savage actions – what we would call uncivilized incidents from our vantage point of progress. *Wuthering Heights* exists outside the mainstream of the English novel; it would be as alien to Thackeray as it was to contemporary reviewers. But it survived his time, as it will survive ours, because imaginative genius transcends convention wherever it is to be found.

A look at some of the great novels of Thackeray's own time shows us just how rich and how great *Vanity Fair* is. The idea that Thackeray was merely an accomplished improviser who, knowing that he was about to achieve great success, succeeded through a kind of inspired exuberance, is false. The number by number publication, far from being a hindrance, was an advantage to a man who had the structure clear in his mind from an early stage, and who was able to look back as he wrote and deepen the tone by subtle repetition and association of character traits, which give the whole novel its ambivalent integrity. Henry James's pronouncement about the loose baggy monsters of nineteenth-century fiction can have no application to *Vanity Fair*. I hope that my close commentary on the number by number publication will have indicated Thackeray's own concern for total relevance. There is a tendency to regard the novel form as relatively unsophisticated (Jane Austen excepted) before the arrival of George Eliot and Henry James on the literary scene. It is critically naïve to believe this: *Vanity Fair* is high art.

Everything subserves the satirical, ironic, compassionate and at times radical view of society which Thackeray displays. A measure of the novel's greatness is our wish to return to it, and every return marks a deepening of experience for the reader. We find, as in Shakespeare, something that we have not seen or fully registered before. Above all, we find that quality of wisdom about life which only the greatest writers possess, and Thackeray needs little defence against the charge of cynicism.

It was fashionable some years ago to refer to *Middlemarch* as a kind of provincial *War and Peace*. *Vanity Fair* is, I believe, a cosmopolitan *War and Peace*, and the wisdom I have referred to above is qualified by a kind of humility. 'Which of us is happy in this world?' asks the author at the end of his novel. The simplicity of that question has a wry sadness about it, which is far from the satirical shafts and the realism through the rest of the novel, yet is a counterpoise to so much of it. It is the other side of ambition, of society, or corrupt aristocratic eminence. It is the still small voice of truth, and that voice, heard between the pages of the novel, gives us a full perspective, not merely on literature, but on life.

Reading List

The following books are recommended to students of *Vanity Fair* who wish to know more about Thackeray's life and works:

BIOGRAPHY The definitive biography, in two volumes, is by Gordon N. Ray: *Thackeray: The Uses of Adversity 1811–1846* (Oxford University Press, 1955). *Thackeray: The Age of Wisdom* (Oxford University Press, 1958). For a fine chapter on *Vanity Fair* see Volume 1 (pp. 384–428).
A readable and well-documented biography is Ann Monsarrat's *An Uneasy Victorian: Thackeray the Man* (Cassell, 1980).

LETTERS *The Letters and Private Papers of W. M. Thackeray* edited by Gordon N. Ray (Oxford University Press, 1945–6). There is no better commentary on Thackeray the man than Thackeray himself; the letters are revealing, warm and vibrant with humour and pathos. Meticulously edited, they provide a fine sense of the times in which the novelist lived.

CRITICISM Geoffrey Tillotson's *Thackeray The Novelist* (Cambridge University Press, 1954) is a perceptive analysis of Thackeray's content and methods.
The Exposure of Luxury: Radical Themes in Thackeray, by Barbara Hardy (Peter Owen, 1972), is particularly strong on *Vanity Fair* (see especially the chapters on 'Art and Nature', 'Rank and Reversal' and 'The Comic Feast').
Thackeray: The Major Novels, by Juliet McMaster (Manchester University Press, 1971), has a particularly good section on 'Narrative Technique: *Vanity Fair*' (pp. 1–49).

TEXTS All quotations in this study are taken from the Penguin English Library edition of *Vanity Fair*, edited by J. I. M. Stewart (Penguin, 1968, reprinted 1983). Other texts which the student will find both helpful and stimulating are:
Vanity Fair edited by Kathleen and Geoffrey Tillotson (Methuen, 1963). This contains a fine introduction and notes.
Vanity Fair edited by John Sutherland (Oxford, The World's Classics, 1983). This edition has a good introduction and notes, complete with Thackeray's own illustrations.

OTHER WORKS OF IMPORTANCE *Thackeray at Work*, by John Sutherland (Athlone Press, 1974), includes an informative and fascinating first chapter on *Vanity Fair*.

Novels of the Eighteen-Forties, by Kathleen Tillotson (Oxford, 1954).
  contains a very good chapter on *Vanity Fair*, noting the 'firm planning
  and complex unity' of it.
The Language of Thackeray, by K. C. Phillipps (André Deutsch, 1978),
  is excellent on the nature and various facets of Thackeray's style.

Appendix: Chronology

The action of *Vanity Fair* covers the years 1813–30, with some gaps and some precisely dated events, domestic and historical. The period of the Regency, during which the Prince of Wales (later George IV) acted as Regent during his father's periodic insanity, lasted from 1811 until 1820, and Thackeray took great care over historical accuracy and period flavour. There are very few errors, though as Kathleen and Geoffrey Tillotson have pointed out in their excellent introduction to the novel, two references properly belong to 1831 – outside the timespan of the novel. These mention Exeter Hall in the Strand, which was opened in that year, and Bellini's *Sonnambula*, which was first produced in 1831.

The novel opens in June 1813, with Amelia and Becky leaving Miss Pinkerton's. The date is 15 June, as we learn from Miss Pinkerton's letter – exactly two years to the day before the Duchess of Richmond's ball. Becky leaves for Queen's Crawley when it is still summer, and is ruling there 'Before she had been a year' in old Sir Pitt's service. This takes us to the summer of 1814, although prior to that there has been an exchange of letters between Mrs Bute and Miss Pinkerton – both dated December, presumably in 1813 – when Mrs Bute is trying to find out all she can about Becky. That Christmas Miss Crawley comes to the Hall, but, as John Sutherland has pointed out, it is difficult to establish how long Becky remains a governess at the Hall, and Christmas 1814 may be intended. The parallel references in the Russell Square chapters (as I shall call them) are factual historical ones – Wellington's victory at Vittoria (June 1813), the terrible French defeat at Leipsic (October 1813), with the invasion of France at the end of the year, Napoleon's abdication in April 1814, and Mr Sedley's 'very grave face' (p. 151) as the shares tumble. Amelia is overjoyed, for George's regiment will not be ordered abroad now that 'the Corsican was overthrown' (p. 151). An illusory period of domestic and international peace sets in.

Becky comes to London with Miss Crawley, and condescends to George Osborne (much to Rawdon's delight), mentioning that she has been at Queen's Crawley for eighteen months, which places us firmly in the early months of 1815, after Miss Crawley's Christmas stay at the Hall. A short period after this, Lady Crawley dies and Sir Pitt proposes to Becky who, we soon learn, has already married Rawdon. A month later she goes to the sale of the Sedleys' belongings and buys the painting of Jos, while the following chapter (18) returns to a wider historical perspective, with the news of Napoleon's landing at Cannes (1 March 1815) – the beginning of the hundred days. The result is the loss of Sedley's fortune 'with that fatal news' (p. 214), while old Osborne writes Amelia the 'brutal letter' (p. 218), breaking off all social intercourse between the families and hence ending her engagement to George.

We can therefore safely date Becky's marriage as occurring in February 1815, while in Chapter 38 (p. 461) we learn that Amelia always keeps her wedding anniversary on 25 April. Ten days after her marriage she is in Brighton on honeymoon (though we learn after her return to see her mother, that she has only been away nine days, a slight but unimportant contradiction). Osborne's dismissive, disinheriting letter to George is dated 7 May. The regiment leaves for Brussels in that month, the Duchess of Richmond's ball, as we have noted, is on 15 June (interestingly, this means that Becky is now twenty-one and Amelia nineteen), and the battle of Waterloo is on 18 June. As John Sutherland has rightly noted, the tight confines of the chronology frustrated Thackeray, and thereafter, with some contradictions, the dates are much more spaced out.

Becky gives birth to little Rawdon on 26 March 1816, in Paris (p. 414), while at this time and during the months preceding it, Pitt is paying Miss Crawley marked attentions. His father is giving himself up to dissolute practices at the Hall with Miss Horrocks. If we return briefly to the post-Waterloo events, Sir William Dobbin goes to see old Mr Osborne with George's last letter (dated 16 June) 'About three weeks after the 18th of June' (p. 417), which places us in the first week of July 1815. By the end of the autumn (presumably October 1815), Osborne visits the battlefield. There he passes by Amelia and Dobbin, but Dobbin comes to see him and speaks of 'Mrs Osborne's condition', telling him that 'She will be a mother soon' (p. 423). The 'soon' is somewhat ambiguous, but it seems idle speculation to imagine that George and Amelia slept together before their marriage (i.e., in April 1815). It is much more likely that little George was conceived during the nine–ten days' honeymoon of late April to early May, and would therefore be born in late January or early February 1816.

There is a terrible irony in the fact that the child is conceived in the pre-Waterloo unhappiness of Amelia, while Becky's child is conceived in the post-Waterloo euphoria. Thackeray's chronology here emphasizes his continuing concern with the contrasting lots of the two women. Specific dates are sparse, but 'twelve months after the above conversation' (i.e., that between old Osborne and Dobbin (p. 424)), Amelia has recovered sufficiently to devote herself to her child (autumn 1816). Dobbin's departure for India can be confidently placed in early August 1816, for we are told that the baby was 'scarcely six months old' (p. 425). Becky and Rawdon would appear to return to London late in 1817, or early in 1818

It is not possible to date Miss Crawley's death, though we know that she dies before their return.

Steyne appears on the scene soon after that return, and ten years later Rawdon is to find banknotes 'dated ten years back' (p. 621). By this time we are firmly in 1827, though once again, with meticulous accuracy, John Sutherland quotes Raggles's words to Becky – 'You've lived in this 'ouse four year' (p. 635) – a contradiction which the reader could be forgiven for missing. There is a reference to little Rawdon being 'five years old' (p. 447), which would place us in 1821; and one summer's day (but when?) he meets little Georgy in the Park. Three days before Georgy's sixth birthday (early in 1822), he is measured for a suit of clothes, the present of Dobbin from India. Meanwhile Sir Pitt's dotage is nearing its end. He dies on 14 September 1822 (p. 480), Becky returns to her 'Ancestral Halls' for the funeral, and Miss Rosalind remarks 'She's hardly changed since eight years' (p. 488) – an accurate reference to Becky's stay there as her nominal governess.

Two pages on we find Thackeray having his customary joke with the reader: 'Fifty years ago, and when the present writer, being an interesting little boy' (p. 490), which would in fact be in 1798, thirteen years before the author was born. This demonstrates a deliberate casualness about dates, a freedom from constriction and a movement towards the expansive narration, which makes incident rightly the foreground, and time almost irrelevant. John Sutherland has put it succinctly when he says:

> This chronological double-dealing also makes believable lecherous Lord Steyne's withholding some eight years (and paying over £1000) before making a serious attempt on Becky's virtue. (*Thackeray at Work*, p. 43)

There are also contradictions in the actual age, at given times, of Rawdon, his son, and old Sir Pitt; while Becky's ancestral visit, mentioned above, has her reflecting on 'her thoughts and feelings seven years back' (p. 496).

Christmas 1822 is spent by Becky and Rawdon at Queen's Crawley, Lady Jane and Becky not getting on '*quite* so well' (p. 530); and there is a neat linking with the way 'Our friends at Brompton' (p. 536) spent theirs. Thereafter, dates become even more vague, mainly because of the Thackerayan technique of going backwards and forwards, using retrospect to bring us up to date, without specifying exactly what that date is. At one stage Becky says to Lady Bareacres, 'I had the pleasure of making your Ladyship's acquaintance at Brussels, ten years ago' (p. 571), which places us in 1825, if Becky's memory is accurate, and we can't be certain about this.

This is the beginning of her triumph in high society. Roughly paralleling this ascent is Amelia's continuing descent; she has to yield up

George to his grandfather, who orders that his son's room should be got ready. We read that in it was 'a dried inkstand covered with the dust of ten years' (p. 579), so that this places little George's arrival in Russell Square as some time in 1825. The 'Sunday after the Battle' chapter is quite obviously set in 1827, since there is a reference, when Rawdon goes to see Macmurdo, to 'His Royal Highness the late lamented Commander-in-Chief' (p. 628). This is the Duke of York, who died in 1827. There is another date in 1827, after Dobbin's return, when Amelia shows him George's essay 'On Selfishness', which bears the date, 24 April 1827. Again we are aware of the brilliantly ironic touch, for it was written on the eve of his mother's wedding anniversary to a husband who symbolized selfishness.

There are about three years between Dobbin's return from India and the Pumpernickel episode, yet the text gives little definite information about the interim, except that Sedley and Osborne both die, and Amelia's position in society is enhanced while Becky's suffers eclipse. We have noted previously that the stay at Pumpernickel is rooted in Thackeray's own experiences in Weimar in 1830–31; but the retrospect on Becky is vague. Thackeray refers to the 'couple of years' (p. 738) which followed the 'Curzon Street catastrophe' (p. 738). We do not know exactly when little Rawdon is made heir to Queen's Crawley. Wenham speaks of little Rawdon as being 'thirteen years old', and says that his mother 'never saw him' (p. 743), thus placing us in 1829 or after; but Becky's various travels are not dated.

There is an interesting reference where 'my little friend Tom Eaves' asserts that he was in Strasburg in 1830 'when a certain Madame Rebecque made her appearance in the opera of the "Dame Blanche"' (p. 748). Steyne's death occurs in 1830 after 'the downfall of the ancient French Monarchy' (p. 753), which occurred in that year. After Dobbin has left, Amelia takes long walks with Georgy in the 'summer evenings' (p. 782). We are told that it 'was June' (p. 784), and that Sir Michael O'Dowd's regiment arrived back on 20 June (p. 784). Later Dobbin is made a Lieutenant-Colonel, and 'after June' (p. 786) Amelia, not caring where she goes but accompanied by Georgy, Becky and Jos, settles in Ostend. From there she writes to Dobbin, and two days later he arrives, quitting the service straight after his marriage. The catalogues of lives and deaths which follow are not given specific dates, for they are in fact the epilogue to the novel's action.

The crisis-point of *Vanity Fair*, which determines the lives of the main characters, has the most specific dating both before and during its action. Thereafter we are caught up in a maze of references, some of them tantalizing, but with the increasing use of retrospect, with the balancing of Becky's lot against Amelia's and their attendant activities, specificity is yielded up in the interests of the narrative sweep, the unfolding of the aftermaths, and the channelling of the tide of history into the stream of domestic crisis. It suited Thackeray's method and it is appropriate to his novel. John Sutherland rightly observes that his success is achieved 'not by more but by less strenuous time-keeping'.

MORE ABOUT PENGUINS, PELICANS AND PUFFINS

For further information about books available from Penguins please write to Dept EP, Penguin Books Ltd, Harmondsworth, Middlesex UB7 0DA.

In the U.S.A.: For a complete list of books available from Penguins in the United States write to Dept DG, Penguin Books, 299 Murray Hill Parkway, East Rutherford, New Jersey 07073.

In Canada: For a complete list of books available from Penguins in Canada write to Penguin Books Canada Ltd, 2801 John Street, Markham, Ontario L3R 1B4.

In Australia: For a complete list of books available from Penguins in Australia write to the Marketing Department, Penguin Books Australia Ltd, P.O. Box 257, Ringwood, Victoria 3134.

In New Zealand: For a complete list of books available from Penguins in New Zealand write to the Marketing Department, Penguin Books (N.Z.) Ltd, Private Bag, Takapuna, Auckland 9.

In India: For a complete list of books available from Penguins in India write to Penguin Overseas Ltd, 706 Eros Apartments, 56 Nehru Place, New Delhi 110019.